W9-AZJ-277

THE WINNING PITCHER

BASEBALL'S TOP PITCHERS DEMONSTRATE WHAT IT TAKES TO BE AN ACE

By TOM HOUSE

CB

CONTEMPORARY
BOOKS

CHICAGO · NEW YORK

Library of Congress Cataloging-in-Publication Data

House, Tom.
    The winning pitcher.

    1. Pitching (Baseball)   I. Title.
GV871.H53   1987   796.357'22   86-32820
ISBN 0-8092-4878-6 (pbk.)

Copyright © 1988 by Thomas House
All rights reserved
Published by Contemporary Books, Inc.
180 North Michigan Avenue, Chicago, Illinois 60601
Manufactured in the United States of America
International Standard Book Number: 0-8092-4878-6

Published simultaneously in Canada by Beaverbooks, Ltd.
195 Allstate Parkway, Valleywood Business Park
Markham, Ontario L3R 4T8 Canada

Contents

THE WINNING PITCHER

1

Why Write a Book on Pitching?

I had some strange ideas during high school, college, and my early years as a professional baseball player. Athletes are often superstitious and those of you who play a sport may understand or see a little of yourself in my idiosyncrasies. They seem funny now, but mastering my false illusions helped me become a better pitcher.

First came my lucky socks era. From the summer of my freshman year in high school until my first year at the University of Southern California, I was convinced that my success as a pitcher came from wearing a pair of white Gold Cup sweat socks. I wore them as part of my uniform under my regular baseball sanitaries, replacing them at least three times over the years. Hard work, short hair (this *was* the early 1960s), no cigarettes, alcohol, or girls (yes, I did succumb to girls, but didn't we all?) were preached by coaches as the formula to becoming a winning athlete. Fine, but it was my lucky Gold Cups that *guaranteed* more wins than losses.

My superstition ended abruptly when my lucky socks failed me during the intersquad games before my first college season. I got tattooed by practically every hitter who stepped into the batter's box—no matter what pitch I threw. They didn't seem to care about the magic of my secret socks.

Shattered, I felt foolish about a system that I thought was infallible. How could I be so naive? I quickly replaced my mental crutch with a physical one, thus beginning my physically fanatic era. I started a fitness/sleep/diet routine that would have put a Spartan soldier to shame—after all, I was a U.S.C. Trojan. I began to believe that the same number of push-ups, sit-ups, wind sprints, the same amount of exercise, pepper and throwing, plus eight hours of sleep, and exactly the same pre-game peanut butter and honey sandwich with two glasses of milk were the reasons I went 34–2 during that time period. Compulsive, yes, but I was better physically conditioned than most of my contemporaries and, because of my small size, it had to help. (I also became a connoisseur of peanut butter—author's choice: Crunchy Jif).

I signed a pro contract with the Atlanta Braves after my sophomore year in college and I realized quickly that my program for staying in shape was not professional baseball's way. Peer pressure and opposing hitters soon made clear the futility of my behavior. Not only was I branded a flake, I found that just working hard wasn't enough to get hitters out consistently. I remember giving up a long home run to a young catcher in Buffalo, New York. As he hit my best curve ball about 450 feet and was rounding the bases, I found myself thinking, "I wonder what he eats before games?" I didn't know that athletes like Johnny Bench can eat anything they want and still hit home runs. Back to the drawing board.

From there, I entered a third stage that I call my "copy Koufax era." Because I was failing professionally, I began to copy any pitcher that was better than me. And since I was terrible, there were plenty of available choices. I thought I'd find the answer in someone else's delivery, pitch selection, grip, aggressiveness—anything but what *I* was doing. But when I tried to throw like Sandy Koufax one start, Denny LeMaster or Juan Marichal the next, I turned in marginal performances. I experimented with forkballs, screwballs, spitballs, cross-seam and no-seam fastballs, knuckle curves, and knuckleballs—all with minimal results. This was, unfortunately, a poor way of matching ability and throwing mechanics to pitch selection; however, I did discover lots of things that *weren't* right for Tom House.

Just when the Braves were ready to give up on me, the minor league farm director really got my attention with this statement: "Show us you can get a left-handed hitter out or this will probably be your last year in organized baseball." Well, even a rockpile

like me could understand that this was my last chance. His *specific* request became my goal, and fear of the lunch pail league broke down all my ego barriers. I re-evaluated my approach to pitching, channeled all my thoughts and efforts toward getting a left-handed hitter out, and ended up on the right track toward major leagues.

This description of my "eras" points out that even with good intentions and instruction (and I had some fine coaches), there is lots of "noise" in the system. Most athletes pick up misinformation or misdirect their efforts at some time in their career. I hope that this book can help pitchers cope with bad information and direction and help them get past those critical times that occur in everyone's playing days.

Baseball is changing and, luckily, I have a front row seat so I can watch our national pastime move from the old school into a new school of theory, technique, instruction, and application. We have all seen the big changes brought about by free agents, big money, owners, and mass media. I am more concerned with quiet, state-of-the-art changes that can influence a pitcher's short- and long-range performance. From sandlot adolescent to established major league star, many things move an athletic career toward success. Looking around, I don't see much written to compare the best of what *was* with the best of what *is*. By "what *was*" I mean baseball's "givens," those things we start with and cannot change. To play the game athletes have to hit, run, throw, and catch on a field where the basepaths are 90', the distance between the rubber and home plate is 60'6", the fences are 300'+ down the line, 400'+ to center. Coaches have players, give them uniforms and equipment, and instruct them with such proven phrases as "weight lifting is bad for pitchers," "bend your back," "don't throw sidearm," "use two hands," or "a pitcher is no better than his legs." I could fill a page with such baseball slogans—all well meant, most fairly correct, but few explaining why they are important.

"What *is*" explains the "why" of baseball's "givens." Medical and technological advances can now explain how baseball's rules work—things that could only be guessed at, or observed through practical experience in the past. Learning time is shortened because information about the athlete's body and mind has grown tremendously in the past decade. In sports medicine, for example, doctors now use arthroscopic surgery to repair injuries and get players back on the field in weeks instead of months. Human performance labs provide data about the interaction of bone, muscle, brain, and nerves that enable athletes to specialize, channeling their efforts to increase their chance of success. Aerobics show that physical conditioning is a programmable, scientific discipline, not a chance result of simply "working out." Biomechanics computerize body positions and movements, providing ideal models for each physical activity (like pitching a baseball). High-speed, stop-action video cameras give us a way to show athletes their performances so that they can compare their good and bad points with the ideal for their position.

Sports psychology is another example of new methods helping athletes to overcome mental barriers that may inhibit their physical performance. Hypnosis, reinforced positive visualization, and other techniques help more and more kids learn to cope with the stresses of being a competitive athlete by teaching ways that their thinking can help their body. I am lucky that my experience, education and interest in helping young athletes succeed in a game (where failure is the rule rather than the exception) has let me bridge the knowledge gap between baseball's old school and new school. Looking back at my early superstitions I realize I was close to a workable formula; it just wasn't in proper perspective. I hope that as you read this book you will find some trail shorteners for yourself or for one of your athletes.

I admit that my approach is different, but a quick biographical sketch may help you understand it. I have always been a "sneaky" left-handed pitcher with an idea. I have invested 27 years from Little League to the major leagues, as both player and instructor. As an amateur, I played in high school, college, and summer leagues. As a professional, I played for the Braves, Red Sox, and Mariners. As an instructor, in addition to being the pitching coach for the Texas Rangers, I've taught pitching for more than 15 years to kids at the San Diego School of Baseball, at local high schools, and, in years past, the minor leagues for the Astros and Padres. Five knee surgeries, numerous shoulder separations, and the minor injuries that are part of the game have given me a solid understanding of physical rehabilitation and how it affects the mind and body of an athlete who depends on his body to make a living. It's a layman's knowledge, but it's practical and firsthand. Many fine doctors repair injured athletes surgically, but few of them can allay the fears or understand the pain of a player trying to regain preinjury form.

Physical conditioning has always been important to me. My body has been an experimental laboratory for the last 15 years. I've tried many things, using some, and learning from all. At 5'9", I have weighed as much as 205 lbs. and as little as 160 lbs., in major league competition. I am a weight trainer and I have tracked the effects of no lifting compared to year-round lifting programs on Nautilus, Universal Gym, Mini-Gym, and free weights. As a runner, I have run little or not at all, and I have trained for, competed in, and finished 10Ks, 13Ks, half marathons, and marathons to stay in condition.

My formal education appears to have little relation to baseball. I have a B.S. in management (primarily a behavioral science degree), an M.B.A. in marketing (a goal-oriented discipline that uses targeting, segmenting, defining objectives and mapping strategies to reach them), and a Ph.D. in sports psychology. Surprising parallels exist between business and baseball with the psychology of stress bridging the gap between the real world and the sports world.

Besides baseball, I've used my formal education in other ways. I've owned and operated three retail stores in San Diego and taught marketing and retailing at San Diego State University during winter semesters for five years.

What does this combination of practical experience, formal education, and occupation add up to? It encouraged me to think about baseball, particularly *pitching* a baseball, in different ways. It helped me stand back and view the game from a distance. It helped free me from a system that perpetuates inconsistencies. I am *for* the game, but not so much *of* the game that I can't see some of its problems and the new ways that can help solve these problems. I have nothing but admiration for old school instructors, but I think that the tools and concepts that they taught with are now outdated. Today we have exciting new ways to help athletes get the most out of their abilities.

Baseball as a system is changing, but the change is slow. "Baseball's way" still dominates with the idea that "It's always been done this way, so it must be right." Many talented and well-meaning people can't see the advantages to new techniques, new ideas. Despite these hard-dying beliefs, there's no denying that interesting parallels

and surprising shortcomings exist in our attempts to guide young athletes toward success at pitching a baseball. For example, teaching in a university demands that a lot of "why" information be presented to go with future practical experience. Teaching on the ball field stresses practical experience and expects the athlete to deal with "why" *after the fact*. There's very little explanation up front. I would like to see coaches tailor a mix of theoretical "whys" and practical experience for each of their pitchers' mental and physical abilities. I think that the best coaches offer *usable* information to help overcome fear of failure. They understand that failing is part of the learning process and if an athlete can learn from failing, he will never be a failure.

Throughout my career, I had coaches yell the phrase "Have an idea!" It didn't take me long to realize that to an old school instructor this means "Don't mess up." I had to figure out, however, how *not* to mess up by *doing just that*. I can't count the number of poorly located fastballs, hung curveballs, or improperly timed change-ups I threw before an "idea" began to form in my head about what would work in those tough situations. "Have an idea" really means get the hitter out in the most efficient way possible.

A new-school instructor should prepare his pitchers with a mental framework *before* game situations arise. Athletes' mental and physical abilities differ, but everyone performs better with a point of reference. I frame this point of reference by thinking through goals, and planning strategy and tactics to reach those goals:

Team Goal: To win (it's implicit).
Personal Goal: To help the team win by doing the job my manager asks me to do. The manager should make the goal clear

by explaining what is expected up front. ("Work him for a ground ball. We need a double play.")

Strategy: To get one hitter out at a time with the best combination of pitches I have for the situation, using location and/or change of speed to best advantage.

Tactics: Use pitches that take advantage of a hitter's weakness. Match what he does best and what he is trying to do in his situation with what you do best and what you want to do in your situation.

The updated version of "Have an idea!" means planning your work and working your plan, giving yourself the best chance at successful pitching. It sounds simple, but it's amazing how many pitchers throw a pitch because it's what the catcher calls, and then wonder why they don't get the job done. "Having lost sight of our objective, we doubled our efforts to get there," sums up what these athletes are doing between the lines. It's not how hard you work but how you direct your hard work that leads to success. In business, strategic planning is one of the most important parts of reaching goals. Without it, there is no direction, and the talents of even the best people are wasted because they cannot channel the effort in a positive direction. It's the same when pitching a baseball—you know you *want* to get him out, but unless you plan *how* to get him out, you won't make best use of your abilities.

I am not and have never been a star athlete. I competed with average tools and a good working knowledge of how to use them. I am very much in awe of the Tom Seavers and Steve Carltons of the game—they are successful and probably intuitively do everything I will talk about in this book. The same goes for the many star pitchers you will see in these pages. They have a natural ability that can't be taught—they just do things right, and their results show it. But there are a lot more people with *my* level of ability than with Seaver's or Carlton's. I *did* pitch in the major leagues for eight seasons. I got hitters out with an 80 mph fastball because I developed an understanding beyond my physical limitations.

I'm going to focus on thought processes and knowledge. I'd like to bring clear, state-of-the-art information to young pitchers so that they know there is nothing magic about pitching a baseball. Since my early years of false illusions, I have learned a lot. I hope I can pass on some of this knowledge so that you can take a shortcut around your own false illusions and learn what it takes to pitch a baseball.

In baseball, (as in life), there are controllable and uncontrollable variables. In pitching, to reach the highest level of achievement your natural ability will allow, you must maximize the controllable variables of physical conditioning, mental conditioning, and the mechanics of the position. This will allow you to cope more effectively with the uncontrollable variables of baseball—the weather, the fans, your teammates, the opposition—in short, the miscellaneous *external* factors.

Your chances of success increase when you control the things you can. By doing this, you are better at coping with uncontrollable variables in the short run, and you can actually influence them in the long run (how your team plays behind you over the course of a season, for example).

Everything in life is uncontrollable if you don't take command of the daily details. There are leaders and followers, but your personality is directable if you remember the biblical phrase, "The Lord helps those who help themselves." If you don't have a strong personality, have the wisdom to follow someone who will take you where you want to go. Being a leader or a follower does not dictate your chances of success. The distinction lies in the decisions you make *while* leading or following. Even mundane decisions have a cumulative effect: where you are now in your career reflects the sum of your daily choices. Evidently, one of your life decisions has been to play or coach baseball, otherwise you probably wouldn't be reading this book. Baseball is only a part of life—even for athletes and instructors who make a career of the game—but it can be an important part of life if you choose that path.

Before you even knew that baseball existed, luck played a part in your exposure to the game—geography, demographics, and psychographics were on your side. How many baseball players do you think there are from the U.S.S.R.? Could their best athletes even hit a baseball? Maybe. Thousands of athletes with potential baseball talent throughout the world never play the game because they are raised in places where baseball is not available to them.

Now let's say you were lucky enough to be exposed to organized baseball and fortunate enough to be blessed with some ability. What if your first experience was totally negative— a bad coach, a team bully, or an injury? That might end it right there. What if you had great ability, your family recognized that ability, and was supportive of your playing,

but your dad's job transferred him to New Zealand? How could you play or gain experience there? Luck and circumstance beyond your control *do* influence career paths. Take heart, however, because many players persevere against incredible odds to achieve success in their sport.

The bottom line is: how strong is your commitment to keep bouncing back from any injury, a poor defensive club, a bad manager, *whatever*? You may not be able to change your *immediate* environment, but you can hang in there until the environment changes. Then you can get back on a path in the direction *you* want to go. This is true wherever you are in your career. Persevering is a "plus" if you remain objective in your critical path choices. Again, *information* must be combined with practical *experience*. If you hit a stone wall, don't beat your head against it. Look for a route to circumvent it and be on your way to other things. If you weigh all the data, personal needs and wants, and then make a decision, it can never be right or wrong—only good or bad. When changes cannot be made, cope and prepare so that you will be ready when opportunity presents itself.

That is about as philosophical as I can get. I still scuffle with things I know are good for me, but that's human nature and it makes life interesting.

Look at the information in this book with an open mind. I had fun writing it, and I hope you enjoy reading it.

2

Physical Conditioning

Baseball has always had its stories about the mythical farm kid who walks ten miles to school every day, hunts with rocks, or throws ripe tomatoes through locomotives. They're favorites of mine—ones I heard first from Boom Boom Beck, an old-timer who helped the Braves pitchers when I was a minor leaguer in the 1960s. "Country strong" is the way many scouts describe a player who is stronger than he looks, but as with many tall tales, this is description based on fact. Many early baseball stars came from the country or farms where long hours and hard work were a way of life. Body strength and physical stamina were necessary to survive, not just attributes that helped performance on the mound. Few athletes today have worked hard physically their whole lives. Ability, size, and the potential for strength and quickness are abundant—but overall physical conditioning is not optimal.

Physical conditioning *is* a function of strength and stamina. For years baseball has *wanted* physically conditioned athletes but shut off many avenues to reaching maximum strength and stamina. Baseball refused to accept the training methods best suited to getting athletes in top shape. Many players grew up with the notion that lifting weights was bad for throwing—that it made pitchers "musclebound." Running anything but sprints was also considered bad. My first year in the big leagues I was discouraged from running distance *and* daily sprints for fear I would have "nothing left in August." Yet, weight training and distance running are two ideal methods for reaching and maintaining peak physical condition. Fortunately, baseball is changing, reluctantly accepting that there are better ways to get in shape than growing up on a farm. New ideas and methods of achieving proper conditioning levels can help maximize an athlete's ability to pitch a baseball.

Strength is created through weight training and weight training is pumping iron, plain and simple. (Picture Arnold Schwarzenegger, Mr. Universe, as an ultimate weight lifter.) Many methods build strength and even more maintain strength once you have gained it, but all building methods have similar principles:

- lift maximum weight with minimum repetitions
- use opposite muscle groups through a full-range motion
- push to muscle failure approximately three times a week
- use a program of maintenance that involves daily work *without* pushing to muscle failure.

With these shared features as a foundation, use the following rules of thumb to guide how and when you should train:

- *stretch* daily
- *build* in the off season
- *maintain* during the season
- *perform* your activity—hitters *swing* a bat, pitchers *throw* a baseball during the season, throw anything in the off season—but throw
- follow a regular training schedule that is best suited to individual time constraints but follow it religiously.

Done properly, weight training should result in increased strength and flexibility. Specificity occurs at times: players who work out on Nautilus will be stronger on those machines than on Universal Gym machines and vice versa. Individual strength on weights or a weight machine depends on the training method used to attain it.

If an athlete has had an injury, physical conditioning should be carefully monitored, especially weight training. The objective is to rebuild strength, but not before the body is ready to accept stress in the injured area. Only then can the injury be stressed—but carefully and with patience to avoid reinjury. Most successful players can push

their bodies and cope with pain, but a high pain threshold during rehabilitation is not desirable. There is a fine line between not enough work and too much. Under a doctor's or physical therapist's care, you can push until it hurts and then back off a notch and perform your workout. Pain from stiffness usually disappears with a proper loosening up/warming up session, but injury pain continues to burn no matter how loose or warmed up you get. An athlete should not be asked to perform if he is hurt; the only exception might be a veteran player who knows his injury, knows his limitations, can perform accordingly, and still get his job done. Young players should never be allowed or forced to perform when hurt.

Finally, weight training for preadolescents should not be done by "pumping iron." During pre-adolescence muscle tissue can be built faster than ligaments, tendons, and bones. A muscle group can actually tear itself off the structure that supports it. Because maturity is reached at different ages, use the "shaving rule" for when a player can begin weight lifting: if you have not had to shave, you don't need to lift. Athletes who are not physically mature enough to lift weights can get results from work against their own bodies by doing push-ups, pull-ups, dips, and sit-ups. A full extension, full range of motion goal must also be used with these exercises.

We have focused primarily on *building* strength, but it is just as important to *maintain* strength once you have gained it. Maintenance programs for in-season work are designed to sustain conditioning peaks achieved during off-season building programs. The biggest difference between building and maintaining is in the intensity of each workout—you don't push to muscle failure in a maintenance program. Because of this, short daily workouts of similar exercises—even on the same machines you normally build on—are possible. Work early in the day so the body can bounce back by practice or game time.

Use your favorite maintenance program system—it doesn't have to be one particular method to be effective. In fact, it is just as efficient to use dumbbells to complement Nautilus or Universal Gym equipment, especially if travel or expense is a factor.

The second component of physical conditioning, stamina, is a measure of bodily efficiency. Stamina shows how well the body performs under sustained periods of cardiovascular and respiratory stress.

Running is probably the best way a pitcher can reach his peak level of stamina. Assuming an athlete is reasonably healthy, doctors say that 25 to 35 minutes three times a week combined with other daily activities is plenty of stamina work. I encourage—notice I say *encourage, not force*—the pitchers I work with to be able to run five miles in 45 minutes or less. I figure that is the most cardiovascular-respiratory stress he will put his body through in a nine-inning game. Running 25 to 35 minutes every other day coupled with throwing, shagging, daily sprint work, and just moving and shagging around the ball field seems to prepare everyone for a weekly five-mile run and works no hardships on starters or relievers—once the commitment is made. There are other ways to build stamina—swimming is about equal to running for physical stress, bike riding offers about half the exertion level for the same length of time, and jumping rope offers about three times the stress level as running in the same time.

What does improved stamina do for a pitcher? Again, it fine tunes the body: the heart distributes blood better, the lungs oxygenate blood better, muscles burn fuel better and longer, and the body generally metabolizes nutrients better. Please do not assume that only pitchers should do stamina work. It is just as important for every player to work on his endurance. Maximizing cardiovascular and respiratory functions in the body is an important goal for every athlete.

Let me mention the importance of recovery time once more. Early-morning physical conditioning allows the body to bounce back for afternoon or evening games. By investing in your body in the morning, you have something to withdraw if the game calls for peak performance that night. Consistent work over the long haul assures that there will always be something to draw on in competition, and it gives you the confidence that your body won't let you down.

Throwing a baseball should be the easiest part of a pitcher's physical routine. Think of a pitcher's body as being a computer. The business principle of G.I.G.O. (garbage in, garbage out) is particularly applicable when trying to throw consistently. If the physical conditioning program you use on your body is garbage, then the results of your pitching efforts will probably be garbage—especially at the level of competition where your ability is truly tested.

A game brings on internal variables that influence physical abilities. Pitchers can throw on the side or in batting practice and never really extend themselves. But put them between the lines against competition, and their physical abilities are put to the test. The body goes into high gear—adrenaline pumps and extraordinary demands are made on muscle, tendon, and bone. (Elbow and shoulder joints stretch as much as a half-inch beyond normal with every pitch!) The body must be ready to handle the extra stress that competition presents.

Short-term chemical and muscular stress during a game should react well with the cumulative, long-term effects of chemical and muscular changes brought on by a good physical conditioning program. Greater durability and pain tolerance are directly related to long-term physical conditioning. This is not a medical discussion, but new studies show that the body can be taught to adapt to stress far beyond what was once considered excessive. Parallels are being discovered about the superhuman feats of athletes in different sports. What, for example, are the common denominators between Mike Marshall appearing in 110 games for the Dodgers in 1974 and Alberto Salazar running a marathon in 2:05? Talent, yes, but just as important, a physical conditioning program that provides a foundation for talent to emerge as performance.

Pitchers have traditionally been pampered with rest to prevent injury and encourage longevity, the idea being that there are only so many pitches in an arm. I disagree. A pitcher who reaches peak physical conditioning and is mechanically sound should be able to throw competitively every day if he is not pushed to muscle failure. When pushed to muscle failure, actual recovery time for each pitcher is the only constraint on the number of, and interval between, his appearances. Starting pitchers in the major leagues throw every four to five days. What I am saying is that tradition forces pitchers to fit into an artificial pitching rotation. It would be smarter to evaluate each pitcher's abilities and find a rotation to make the most of them. The only limitations should be ability and willingness to work to find the best interaction between physical conditioning and ability level.

A side note: I pitched a game for the Seattle Mariners against Jon Matlack when he was with the Texas Rangers. Arlington Stadium has a large electronic scoreboard and flashes a "fastest pitch last inning" speed in miles per hour after every inning. The first inning (on a typical hot, humid Dallas day), his fastest was 92 mph, mine was 82 mph. After the last inning of the game, his best was 84, mine was still 82. He beat us 2–1 as his ability probably dictated, but if I had lost the same relative velocity, I wouldn't have gotten into the third inning. (I figure he would have reached my velocity level in two more innings and that physical conditioning was the difference!)

Arms are often injured in the deceleration phase of throwing because three muscle groups accelerate the arm but only one slows it down. Knowing this, a young pitcher should start a lifting and maintenance program to push arm strength and flexibility beyond, or at least equal to, the level of stress his arm endures during a game. If you accept this, there is no set number of pitches in an arm—only a set amount of willingness to work to find the greatest strength and flexibility. Muscle memory and muscle tissue reaction are unique to each body but they can be monitored. I hope that by breaking away from traditional thinking, tradition itself will no longer stop a pitcher from maximizing his potential.

Striving for peak physical conditioning is the first step toward succeeding as a pitcher. The old expression "preparation meets opportunity" is true here. Good physical condition doesn't guarantee success, but it does set a foundation to build on—one that won't cave in during physical stress. It's the first controllable variable on our road to success, the path toward achieving the best results from our physical efforts as pitchers.

3

The Complete Pitcher's Workout

We've just talked about physical condition-ing, a variable that can be controlled through good exercise habits and discipline. In this chapter, you'll find practical infor-mation on stretching, sit-ups, strength-training, running, and nutrition.

STRETCHING

Stretching should be done slowly with no bouncing or jerky movements. Do slight, easy stretches and hold them for 15 to 30 seconds, then slowly increase the stretch as you feel comfortable. Do not strain a stretch that is painful. Stretch your muscles slowly and with control, remembering that the key is to be relaxed.

Try to work these stretches into your daily workout routine. They'll keep your muscles from stiffening, and help to prevent injury.

1. Relax with your knees bent and the soles of your feet together. This will stretch your groin. Hold for five seconds.

2. Lying on your back, bring your knees together and rest your feet on the floor. Clasp your hands behind your head and rest your arms on the mat. Using your arms, slowly bring your head, neck, and shoulders forward until you feel a slight stretch. Hold for five seconds. Repeat.

3. Beginning in the same position, lift the left leg over the right leg. From here, use your left leg to pull your right leg to-ward the floor until you feel a good stretch in your leg. Keep the upper back, shoulders, and elbows flat on the floor. Hold for 30 seconds. Repeat stretch for other side.

4. Straighten both legs, then pull your left leg toward your chest, keeping the back of your head on the mat. Hold for 30 seconds. Repeat.

5. Bend one knee, and with your opposite hand pull that bent leg up and over your other leg. Keep both your shoulders on the floor. With your hand on your thigh, control the stretch in your lower back and butt muscles by pulling your upper leg down toward the floor. Repeat the

stretch to your other side. Hold stretch for 30 seconds on each side.

6. Lie on your back with your legs over-head, knees bent, and hands on the back of your hips for balance. Find a comfortable position and hold for 30 seconds.

7. From the legs-overhead position, roll down slowly, trying to lower one verte-bra at a time. Put your hands directly behind your knees and keep your legs bent as you roll down. Be sure to keep the back of your head on the floor or mat.

8. Sitting upright, put the soles of your feet together. With your hands around your feet, pull yourself forward to stretch your groin and back. Do not bounce. Hold for 30 seconds.

9. With your legs in front of you and your heels about four inches apart, bend over at the waist and try to touch your toes. Don't bounce. Hold for 30 seconds.

10. With your right leg straight, put your left foot flat on the other side of your right knee. Reach over your left leg with your right arm so that your elbow is on the outside of your left leg. With your left hand resting on the ground behind you, slowly turn your head to look over your left shoulder, and, at the same time, turn your upper body (but not your hips) toward your left hand and arm. Hold for 10 seconds for each side.

11. In a sitting position, open your legs as wide as possible. With your legs straight and feet relaxed at the ankles, slowly lean forward at the hips until you feel a good, even stretch on the inside of the upper legs. Keep your back straight. Hold for 30 seconds.

12. To stretch your left hamstring and the right side of your back, slowly bend forward from the hips toward the foot of your left leg. Keep your head forward and back straight. Hold for 30 seconds on each side.

13. Sit up and place the leg which you have been stretching behind you in the hur-dle stretch position. Slowly lean back to stretch your quads further. Hold for one minute.

14. Straighten your bent leg and bring the sole of your other foot to rest next to the inside and upper part of your straight-ened leg. Lean forward slightly and stretch the hamstrings of the leg that is straight in front of you. Find an easy stretch and relax. Hold for one minute.

15. With your feet shoulder width apart and pointed out to about a 45-degree angle, bend your knees and squat down. If you have trouble staying in this posi-tion, hold onto something for support. It is a great stretch for your ankles, ten-dons, groin, and lower back. Hold for 30 seconds.

16. To stretch your calf, stand a little way from a wall and lean on it with your forearms, resting your head on your hands. Bend one leg and place your foot on the ground in front of you, leaving the other leg straight out behind you. Slowly move your hips forward until you feel a stretch in the calf of your straight leg. Be sure to keep the heel of the foot of the straight leg on the ground and your toes pointed straight ahead. Hold for 30 seconds. Do not bounce. Stretch both legs.

17. A stretch for the arms, shoulders, and back. Hold onto something that is about shoulder height. With your hands shoulder width apart on this support, relax, keeping your arms straight, your chest moving downward, and your feet remaining directly under your hips. Hold this stretch for 30 seconds.

18. Another stretch for the shoulders and arms can be felt by holding onto a fence

or both sides of a doorway with your hands behind you at about shoulder level. Let your arms straighten as your body leans forward, keeping your chest and head up. Hold stretch for 15 seconds.

19. Grab one elbow with the opposite hand and gently pull elbow behind your head. This will stretch the back of your arm and shoulder. Hold for 15 to 20 seconds.

20. Next, with your arms extended overhead, grab one hand with the other and pull your arm over your head as you bend sideward at the waist. Do not try to go too far. This is a good stretch for your shoulders, sides, and back of upper arm. Hold this stretch for 5 to 15 seconds.

A SIT-UP PROGRAM FOR MAINTENANCE WORK

Designed to work all muscle groups in abdominal area. Low back is always supported—no disc or nerve problems should occur if properly executed.

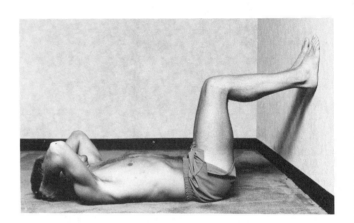

Exercise #1
Lie on floor close enough to a wall so feet are flat against the wall and knees are bent at a 90-degree angle. Put hands behind head and lift upper body until elbows reach knees—alternate right elbow to left knee, etc., keeping feet flush against the wall.

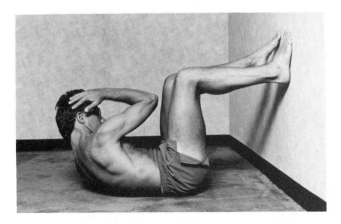

Exercise #2

Lie on floor close enough to a wall so legs and bottom are flush to surface of wall. Clasp hands together and reach to full extension over top of head. Lift upper body off ground and touch hands as high as possible on legs, keeping lower body flush to wall.

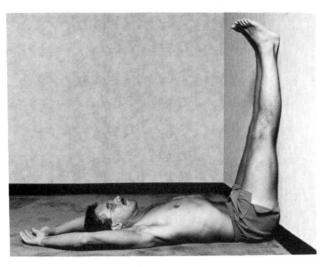

Exercise #3

Lie on floor with hands clasped behind head and legs bent at the knees (at an angle that permits low back and bottom of feet to be flat on floor). Lift upper body as high as possible off the floor, keeping hands behind head, lift lower body until knees touch elbows and then return upper body to floor, followed by lower body until original position is reached.

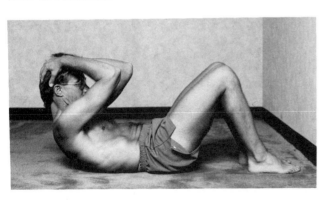

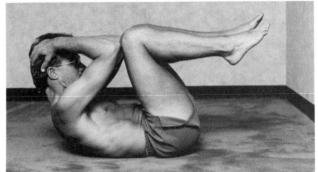

Exercise #4
Start in same position as in exercise #3. Lift upper and lower body simultaneously to where elbows touch knees, then return to original position.

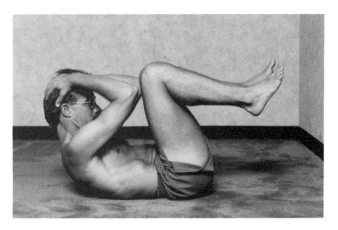
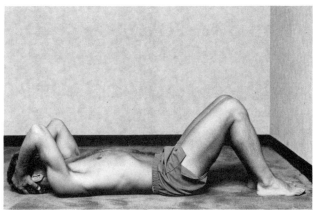

Exercise #5
Start in same position as in exercises 3 and 4. Lift upper body as high as possible, then lower body until elbows touch knees at that point. Extend legs and arms, trying to grab ankles with hands. Then return upper body to floor followed by lower body until original position is reached.

Exercise #6
Start in same position as in exercises 3, 4, and 5. Lift *lower* body until legs and knees are at a 90-degree angle. Lift upper body until elbows touch knees. Bicycle legs with elbows touching opposite knees until fatigued and return to original position.

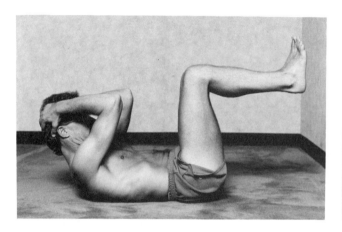

STRENGTH TRAINING PROGRAM

This program is divided into three parts: a power training program to build your strength; shoulder and arm exercises to help maintain your rotator cuff and avoid injuries; and a revolutionary "underloading" technique that is changing the way major league pitchers are conditioning their arms and practicing their pitching.

Power Training Program

This program, developed by Dr. Thomas McLaughlin for the United States Olympic Committee Sports Medicine Council's book, *Injuries to the Throwing Arm*, is a year-round weight program designed to build body strength and power. The program is divided into four phases. The first phase, which begins in the off-season, is the "base" cycle, lasting ten weeks. During this time, you'll be developing muscle strength and hypertrophy. Once this cycle has been completed, you'll spend nine weeks in a "power" cycle (also in the off-season), in which the intensity of your weight work increases until you are doing only two reps per set. As a result, your performance (in terms of power production) will peak just as the season begins.

The third part of the program is the "maintenance" phase, which lasts throughout the season. This will help to prevent any significant losses in the strength and power you developed before the season began. Finally, in the fourth phase, it's important to spend three weeks "actively" resting; that is, you engage in other activities beside baseball and weight training.

In terms of specific training methods, take a look at Tables A, B, and C. These will give you sample exercises for the base cycle, the power cycle, and the maintenance phase. Also, note Figure 1, which gives the repetitions you should use during different stages of the cycle.

TABLE A. SAMPLE PROGRAM FOR BASE CYCLE 1

MONDAY		WEDNESDAY		FRIDAY
Exercises	**Intensity***	**Exercises**	**Intensity**	
(1) Wide grip bench press	(100%)	(1) Medium stance squats	(100%)	(1) Same exercises as in Monday workout, except that no squats are performed
(2) Wide grip bent rowing	(100%)	(2) Wide grip high pulls	(100%)	
(3) Lying triceps press	(100%)	(3) Wide grip shrugs	(100%)	
(4) Concentration curl	(100%)	(4) Back extensions	(100%)	(2) Intensity is 85% for all exercises.
(5) Dumbbell press	(100%)	(5) Abdominal curl-ups	(100%)	
(6) Shoulder laterals	(100%)	(6) Dumbbell chest flies	(70%)	
(7) Barbell T-bench press	(100%)	(7) Wide grip lateral pulls to chest	(70%)	
(8) Medium stance squats	(50%)	(8) Shoulder laterals	(70%)	
(9) Abdominal curl-ups	(50%)	(9) Forearms (optional)	(70%)	
(10) Forearms (optional)	(100%)			

TABLE B. SAMPLE PROGRAM FOR POWER CYCLE 2

MONDAY		WEDNESDAY		FRIDAY
Exercises	**Intensity***	**Exercises**	**Intensity**	
(1) Dumbbell bench press	(100%)	(1) Wide stance (outside shoulder width squats)	(100%)	(1) Same exercises as in Monday workout, except that no squats are performed
(2) Dumbbell bent rowing	(100%)			
(3) Close grip (approximately 6") bench press	(100%)	(2) Medium grip high pulls	(100%)	(2) Intensity is 85% for all exercises.
(4) Supinating dumbbell curl	(100%)	(3) Medium grip shrugs	(100%)	
(5) Dumbbell press	(100%)	(4) Back extensions	(100%)	
(6) Shoulder laterals	(100%)	(5) Abdominal curl-ups	(100%)	
(7) Dumbbell T-bench press	(100%)	(6) Dumbbell chest flies	(70%)	
(8) Wide stance outside (shoulder-width) squats	(50%)	(7) Medium grip lateral pulls to chest		
(9) Abdominal curl-ups	(50%)	(8) Shoulder laterals	(70%)	
(10) Forearms (optional)	(100%)	(9) Forearms (optional)	(70%)	

*Intensity is based on the amount of weight the athlete can lift for a required set and repetition combination. For example, 100 per cent means that the maximal weight used is that which permits performance of all three sets of whatever repetitions are used.

TABLE C. SAMPLE PROGRAMS FOR MAINTENANCE (IN SEASON)

(1) First 10 Weeks		(2) Second 10 Weeks	
Day One	**Day Two**	**Day One**	**Day Two**
(1) Squats (¼ only) medium stance*	(1) Squats, medium stance	(1) Outside shoulder stance squats	(1) Outside shoulder stance squats
(2) Wide grip bench press	(2) Wide grip high pulls	(2) Dumbbell bench press	(2) Medium grip shrugs
(3) Wide grip bent rowing	(3) Concentration curls	(3) Dumbbell bent rowing	(3) Dumbbell press
(4) Dumbbell press	(4) Lying triceps press	(4) Shoulder laterals	(4) Twist curls
(5) Back extensions	(5) Shoulder laterals	(5) Back extensions	(5) Close grip bench press
(6) Abdominal curl-ups	(6) Barbell T-bench press	(6) Abdominal curl-ups	(6) Dumbbell T-bench
(7) Forearms (optional)	(7) Abdominal curl-ups	(7) Forearms (optional)	(7) Abdominal curl-ups
	(8) Forearms (optional)		(8) Forearms (optional)

*Intensity for the entire maintenance program is approximately 70 to 85 per cent for all exercises.

FIGURE 1

"BASE" CYCLE 1 → "POWER" CYCLE 2 → MAINTENANCE → "ACTIVE" REST

(10 WEEKS)
(1) 3 weeks-10 reps
(2) 2 weeks-5 reps
(3) 3 weeks-10 reps
(4) 2 weeks-5 reps

(9 WEEKS)
(1) 3 weeks-10 reps
(2) 3 weeks-5 reps
(3) 2 weeks-3 reps
(4) 1 week-2 reps

(30 WEEKS)
(1) moderate W weights. 3-5 reps
(2) change exercises every 10 weeks

(3 WEEKS)
participate in other recreational sports.

In order to fully benefit from this program, it's important to keep these things in mind:

- The exercises in Tables A, B, and C should be followed in the order presented here, with the compound, larger muscle mass exercises coming earlier in the workout.
- Use only free weights, particularly dumbbells whenever possible, since they offer greater freedom of movement.
- Always do a pre-workout warm-up, which includes flexibility work followed by light, total body exercises (three sets of ten reps using only the bar for light cleans and jerks).
- Each exercise should begin with one light to moderate warm-up, using the same number of reps you'll be doing at full weight.
- Always do three sets, with two minutes rest between sets.
- Poundage used on the 100% intensity days should be increased whenever possible as long as good technique isn't sacrificed. Poundage used on lighter intensity days should be scaled upward proportionately.
- In all these exercises, your movement should be as "explosive" as possible, to work as closely as possible to the force/velocity curve.
- End each workout with a "cooldown," letting your muscles stretch and recover from your workout.

Shoulder and Arm Exercises

These exercises were developed by the very famous Dr. Frank Jobe, who has restored the arms of countless pitchers (as well as the bodies of many, many professional athletes). Dr. Jobe's extensive research into the movements of pitchers has led him to recommend the following exercises for all pitchers, no matter what level you play at. Following his program closely will help you protect that all-important rotator cuff and avoid injury to your arm.

Stretching the Rotator Cuff
Rotator Cuff Stretch at 90°
The capsule around the shoulder joint needs to be stretched before maximum movement can be obtained. Begin these exercises on a table with a small weight in your hand. Your shoulder should be over the table edge and elbow bent to 90°. Just allow the weight to pull your arm down gently in this position.

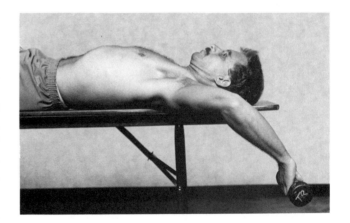

Rotator Cuff Stretch with Arm at 135°
During static flexibility exercises, a particular position is held for a period of time. Static stretching is the best way to initiate a sequence. After stretching, a muscle can be gently moved through this range of motion. In this exercise, raising your arm another 45° stretches more of the tissue surrounding the shoulder.

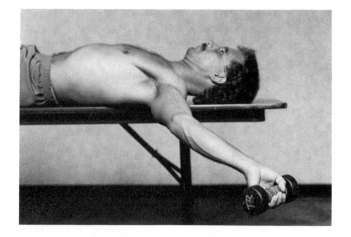

Rotator Cuff Stretch with Arm Overhead
Finally, this exercise should be repeated with your arm as far overhead as possible. Your head should remain supported while the shoulder itself is over the table edge. Again, just allow the weight to pull your arm down gently.

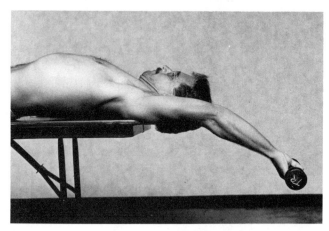

Posterior Cuff Stretch
The back portion of the shoulder joint can be stretched out in this position by gently pulling your arm across your body.

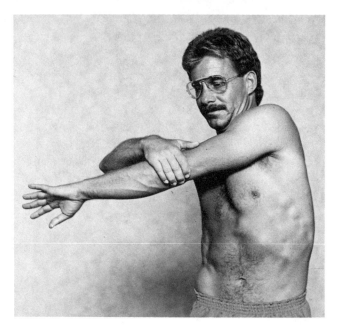

Interior Cuff Stretch

The other portions of the rotator cuff can be stretched by reaching overhead and gently pulling on your elbow with the opposite hand.

Strengthening the Shoulder Muscles

Although it may not seem to take enormous strength to throw a baseball, conditioning and endurance are still necessary. The strengthening exercises you will see in the next few photos can be started with just a few pounds of weight and increased as time goes on.

Supraspinatus

The rotator cuff in the shoulder needs to be strengthened separately from the other shoulder muscles. This first exercise should be done with the elbow straight and thumb turned toward the floor. Rather than putting the arm straight out to the side, slowly raise your arm in a plane about 30° forward of that posture. Do not lift your arms higher than just below shoulder level; slowly lower it to the starting position and repeat.

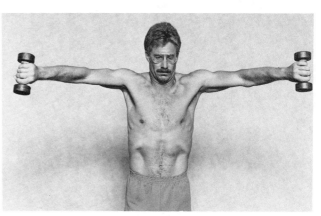

External Rotation

Another part of the rotator cuff can be strengthened by lying on your side with your elbow held close against your ribs. Slowly raise the weight until it is pointed at the ceiling, and then lower it in a controlled fashion.

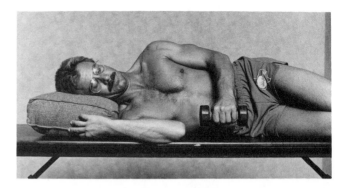

Shoulder Flexion

This particular exercise strengthens a portion of the deltoid as well as other muscles in the front of the shoulder. In this and in succeeding exercises, it is important to move the weights slowly, controlling both the lifting and lowering. The elbow should be kept straight throughout the exercise.

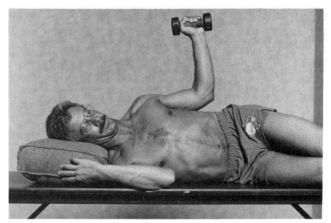

Internal Rotation

The other portion of the rotator cuff should be exercised while lying on your back. Again, with your arm held at the side, raise the weight until it is pointed toward the ceiling, and then lower it slowly back to the starting position.

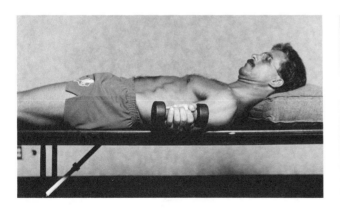 

Shoulder Abduction

Lifting the weight out to the side and then overhead strengthens the central part of the deltoid, which is one of the most powerful muscles in the shoulder. Note how the hand slowly changes position as the exercise progresses until the palm faces the opposite side as your arm reaches straight overhead.

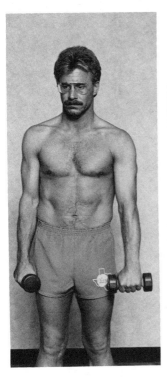

Strengthening the Trunk Muscles
Rhomboids
Back muscles are also important in throwing. Lying on your stomach, grasp the weight firmly and raise it up until your arm is straight out to the side, keeping the elbow extended. Slowly lower it to the starting position.

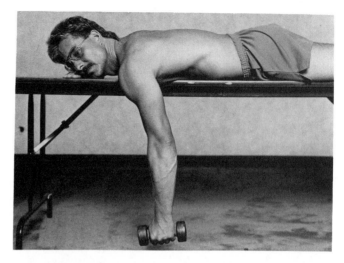

Trapezius
To strengthen muscles lower in your back, remain in the same position on the table and, this time, raise your arm behind you as high as possible, remembering to keep your elbow straight.

Pectoralis Major

The pectoralis is also important in carrying the arm forward. Lie on your back, hold a weight in your hand, and move your arm up until your hand is toward the ceiling. Keep your elbow straight. Do a set slowly and then a set more quickly to imitate the speed of your arm during a throw.

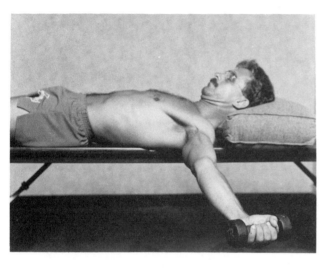 

Latissimus Dorsi

This muscle fires at its maximum during the last half of the pitching motion, contributing power. It can be exercised by attaching some surgical tubing overhead and then pulling down and across your body.

Strengthening the Forearm and Elbow
Elbow Flexion

The muscles in the arm which surround the wrist and elbow must be strengthened as well. The biceps can be exercised in a number of ways, one of which is demonstrated here in the standing position. Keeping the elbow held at the side and the palm toward the ceiling, lift the weight slowly by bending the elbow. By controlling the return part of the exercise, you really do a second exercise. We know that the biceps works most in pitching during the follow-through portion of the throw to slow down the rapid extension of the elbow. So, pay special attention to the straightening portion of the movement.

Forearm Supination

The musculature of the forearm and wrist plays an important part in the ultimate control of the ball. To strengthen the forearm, two separate exercises can be done. First, while seated at a table and holding a bar weighted at one end, rotate your forearm until the bar is pointed at the ceiling.

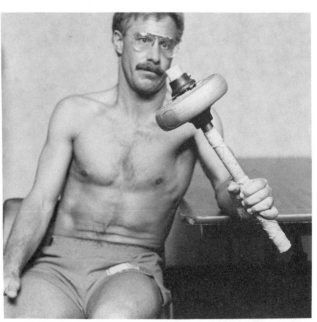

Forearm Pronation

The second forearm exercise is also done while seated, only this time with palm turned up while holding onto the weighted bar. Rotate the bar from right to left, until it is pointed straight up to the ceiling. Pay some attention to keeping your elbow as motionless as possible.

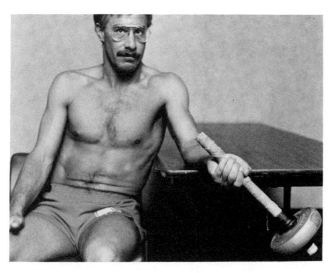 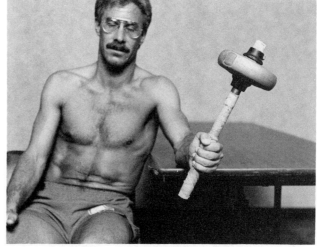

Triceps

Pitchers use the triceps to drive the elbow forward during acceleration. To exercise the triceps muscle, lie on your back with your throwing arm extended up toward the ceiling, elbow completely flexed. Use your opposite hand to help support your arm, just below the elbow. Then, extend the elbow completely while holding a weight.

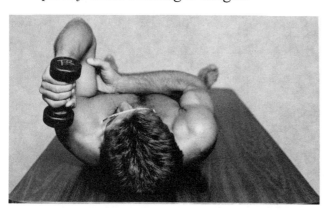 

Strengthening the Wrist
Wrist Flexion
There are several exercises which can help strengthen the wrist muscles. This one is done while seated, with the forearm supported on the table and the wrist over the edge, palm facing up. Use the opposite hand to help stabilize the forearm. Lift the weight slowly, flexing the wrist, and then lower the weight back to the starting position.

 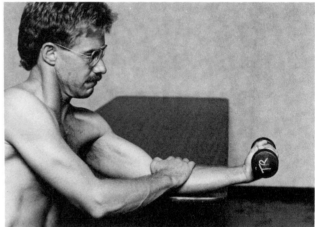

Wrist Extension
While in the same position as the previous exercise, this time turn the palm down toward the floor. Lift the weight by extending the wrist, and then lower it back to the original position.

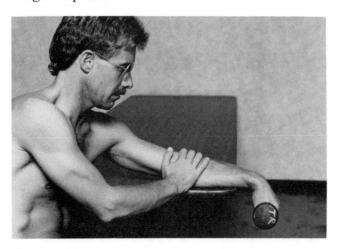 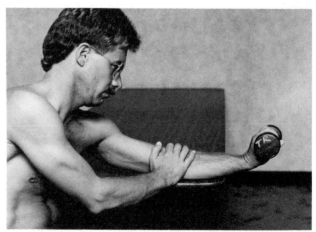

Ulnar Deviation
To strengthen the muscles which control the side to side motion occurring at the wrist, stand with your arm at your side, holding onto the end of a weighted bar. Lift the weight as shown here by bending the wrist laterally. Return slowly to the starting position.

These exercises should be done daily. Begin the program by doing two sets of 10 each, using a light (two-pound) weight for resistance. The amount of weight can be increased later, but this should be done gradually so that it does not cause soreness.

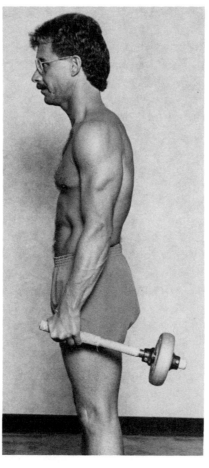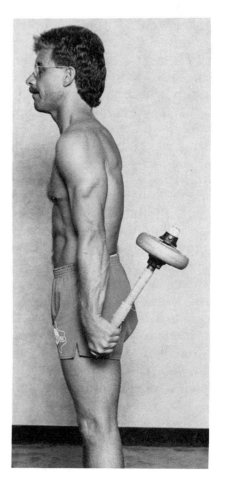

Implement Weight Training: Underloading and Overloading

Weight training for strength and speed is obviously essential, but it's just as essential that your training program is geared for the sport you play, in this case baseball, and more specifically, pitching. It's important that the way you train enhances the exact movements you must make as a pitcher, as well as accommodate the fluid coordination and competitive speed you require. In other words, your weight training program should be designed to make you a more accurate, durable pitcher, and not merely a bigger and more muscular athlete. Therefore, you should be supplementing your training program with specific exercises incorporated into your regular training regimen.

The term "specific" here relates to those exercises that directly affect the way you pitch a baseball. Accordingly, the exercises must be compatible with a pitcher's accelerating and decelerating arm movements. The state-of-the-art program that provides these benefits is called *implemental weight training*. Implemental weight training consists of exercises that use modified baseballs (lighter or heavier baseballs). As you go through the identical full range of motion that you would if you were using a standard baseball, your fast-twitch muscle fiber in your arm will actually produce increases in your veolcity. Why? Because you are not only exercising the muscles; you are also causing neurological changes, since you are throwing at the same velocity as you would a regular baseball. This is called overloading/underloading. You are actually conditioning your muscle memory to believe that you are still throwing the lighter ball, your muscles work faster, and therefore, you'll be increasing the velocity with which you throw.

This revolutionary approach to pitching was developed by Dr. Coop DeRenne of the University of Hawaii and me, and while it's just beginning to get recognition in the major leagues, there's no doubt that this technique is indeed the wave of the future for pitchers of all levels.

RUNNING PROGRAM

This is a simple, eight-week training program designed to get you in shape for a five-mile run. I'm assuming that you're in reasonably good physical condition. If not, build a gradual fitness base with walking, then jogging, before starting week one.

Weeks 1 and 2 (6 miles each week)
Sunday: 1–2 mile run, steady
Monday: Rest
Tuesday: 1-mile jog
Wednesday: Some light walking
Thursday: 2 miles, jogging and walking
Friday: 1-mile jog
Saturday: Some light walking

Weeks 3 and 4 (9 miles each week)
Sunday: 2–3 mile run, steady
Monday: Rest
Tuesday: 2 miles, jogging and walking
Wednesday: 1-mile jog
Thursday: 2 miles, steady
Friday: 1-mile jog
Saturday: Some light walking

Weeks 5 and 6 (12 miles each week)
Sunday: 3–4 mile run, steady
Monday: Rest
Tuesday: 2-mile jog
Wednesday: 1-mile jog
Thursday: 3 miles, jogging and walking
Friday: 2-mile jog
Saturday: Some light walking and jogging

Weeks 7 and 8 (15 miles each week)
Sunday: 4-mile run, steady
Monday: Rest
Tuesday: 3 miles, jogging and walking
Wednesday: 2-mile jog
Thursday: 3 miles, steady
Friday: 2-mile jog
Saturday: 1-mile jog

EAT TO COMPETE

During my years as a pitcher, from Little League through college ball, I was told to run a lot. This was to have strong legs for those late innings, to keep me from running out of gas on the mound. Nothing, however, was ever mentioned about what type of fuel I should put into my body to complement the running.

Today we know that the running is important for its cardiovascular effect—to increase strength and stamina by increasing blood flow and oxygen to the muscles. We have also learned through research that, in effect, "you are what you eat." A person cannot think well or work well if he has not eaten well.

A good analogy compares your body to an automobile. To make it run efficiently, it must be fueled with the best possible gas and oil. Likewise, your body must have the purest blood circulating to its movable parts. The composition of the blood depends on the food we eat. If you eat properly, normal blood is generated and the heart, liver, other organs, and muscles function as they should. Under these conditions, inefficiency is practically impossible. If you take two pitchers of equal ability, with the same workout program, the one most conscientious about his diet will have more energy to sustain peak performance levels. Why? A skilled athlete must have good timing, accuracy of movement, and the proper degree of muscular tension during competition. For a muscle to contract, it must have an energy source called ATP. In the presence of oxygen, the muscle gets all the ATP it needs. The supply of oxygen in a muscle is solely a function of blood flow through the tissue so if blood flow is restricted for any reason, muscle fatigue results.

Five Factors that Contribute to Muscle Fatigue

1. Food allergies.
2. Enzyme deficiency.
3. Refined carbohydrate, protein, and fat ingestion before competition.
4. Anaerobic exercise to excess—calisthenics, sprinting, weight lifting.
5. A training schedule that is too vigorous and does not allow muscle recovery.

Four Factors that Contribute to Muscle Contraction

1. Compatible foods.
2. Adequate enzyme intake.
3. Complex carbohydrates.
4. Aerobic exercise—jogging, swimming, bicycling, jumping rope.

During the last decade, doctors discovered that food allergies can cause symptoms in many parts of the body. They've also found that these symptoms can be dramatically relieved when one or more allergy-producing foods are eliminated from the diet. Another interesting phenomenon is that the foods that cause a child's symptoms are often his favorites—he may crave them and eat them several times a day!

St. Louis allergist Dr. William Bryan developed a test for food allergies that studies the impact of the allergy-causing substance on the white blood cells, our body's defense system against disease. He found that the food reaction seen in the white blood cells aggravates most illnesses. Those foods that destroy an athlete's white blood cells should be eliminated from his diet.

The Two Types of Food Allergies

1. A fixed or permanent allergy is usually caused by uncommon foods like strawberries, lobster, or shrimp. Skin rashes, hives, or other violent skin eruptions are typical of this type of allergic reaction. Common foods like chocolate, eggs, or peanuts can sometimes cause the same problems.
2. A hidden or variable allergy, while more common, is harder to recognize and is often overlooked. Characteristic symptoms of such allergies include fatigue, irritability, pale color, dark circles under the eyes, stuffy nose, stomachache, headache, leg ache, and mouth-breathing. Foods commonly involved with such reactions include milk, corn, chocolate, wheat, egg, cane sugar, citrus fruits, beans, beef, and pork. (It's no wonder they're overlooked!)

Remember this: when diet is deficient, allergy and illness are apt to occur.

When food is cooked above 118 degrees Fahrenheit, the enzymes are destroyed. This means that the pancreas, salivary glands, stomach, and intestines must come to the rescue and *furnish* digestive enzymes to break down protein, carbohydrates, and fats in cooked foods. Eventually, there will be a deficiency of enzymes because the body must rob enzymes from glands, muscles, nerves, and blood to help in the chemical breakdown of food. Many researchers feel that this enzyme deficiency is the real cause of allergies and disease.

Cooked food passes more slowly through the digestive tract than raw food, and, as a result, can set up allergic reactions including gas, heartburn, headaches, stuffy nose, and eye problems. The best natural source of digestive enzymes would come from eating raw vegetables *with* cooked foods. Pineapple and papaya are excellent sources of enzymes to work on proteins. Aspergillus plants have the enzymes to help digest protein, fats, and carbohydrates.

Refined carbohydrates should be avoided or at least limited at mealtime, including sugar in the sugar bowl, candy, soft drinks, cookies, doughnuts, and most junk foods. Some of the foods Mom thought were good for you—such as peanut butter, ketchup, breakfast cereals, and many canned fruits and vegetables—also have hidden sugar. This sugar gets into the bloodstream rapidly giving the body a quick burst of energy, but one that doesn't last long. After a short time, the body becomes jittery and suffers a letdown of muscle fatigue—actually to a point lower than before the food was eaten. This becomes a problem for the person who eats a second round of refined carbohydrates for another quick pickup, as the cycle repeats itself.

Complex carbohydrates, on the other hand, contain time-released sugar. Because this sugar comes into the bloodstream gradually, the body's muscles work better because energy is sustained over a longer period of time. This gives a pitcher the fuel to perform a full nine innings.

Some Sources of Complex Carbohydrates

1. Whole grain flours, such as whole wheat, buckwheat, cornmeal, rye.
2. Grains such as brown rice, buckwheat, barley, cracked wheat.

3. Cereals such as millet, oats, shredded wheat, bran, wheat germ, plain granola.
4. Legumes such as peas, beans, lentils.
5. Potatoes.
6. Pasta made with whole wheat, soy, or semolina flours.

Remember that the body burns carbohydrates first, then proteins or amino acids. The best sources of animal protein include meat, fish, poultry, eggs, milk, and milk products. Good sources of plant protein include soybeans, peas, beans, and nuts. Because animal protein takes a long time to digest, it should be avoided the night before and the day of a pitching performance. Eat protein *after* the performance to help muscles build and repair themselves.

What Is Oxygen Debt?

Fat is burned by the body, and is the major cause of oxygen debt. To burn fat effectively, an athlete must exercise aerobically. An aerobic exercise is one that:

1. is steady and non stop;
2. lasts about 20 minutes;
3. maintains the pulse rate at 70 percent to 80 percent of the maximum during the exercise;
4. should be done every other day.

If a player is not exercising properly, the oxygen supply to his muscles is inadequate, and his body performs sluggishly. The portion of the fuel that is not burned completely is called lactic acid and it impedes muscle contraction, increases fatigue, and eventually causes cramping. Fat can have four times as many blood vessels as an equivalent amount of muscle tissue, so excess fat really puts a strain on the heart. Fat intake comes from meat, dairy products, oils, nut butters, avocados, and olives. Eating too much fat can cause obesity, skin problems, hypoglycemia, diabetes, and many other disease symptoms.

The primary signs of oxygen debt are labored breathing and panting. When this happens, the athlete is exercising anaerobically, and getting no benefit from his workout program.

What Foods Should or Shouldn't Be Eaten During Training?

1. Do *not* eat sugar or sugar substitutes, refined carbohydrates, canned foods, fried foods, alcoholic beverages, coffee, or tea.
2. Do eat from the four basic food groups, including meat, milk, eggs, fruit, vegetables, nuts, and whole grain breads and cereals.
3. Eat a good high-protein breakfast to stabilize the blood sugar level and a moderate low-fat lunch of complex carbohydrates and some protein. The evening meal should be lightest, consisting mainly of complex carbohydrates.
4. Take a good multivitamin/mineral supplement to balance nutritional loss from poor soil, transportation, storage, processing, preparation.

What Should a Pitcher Eat on Game Days?

1. Eat three hours before the game if possible. The meal should be high in complex carbohydrates—brown rice, potatoes, pasta, or cooked cereals—and low in protein because proteins are not easily burned. Stay away from fats, oils, or refined carbohydrates—no butter, whole milk, cheese, salad oil, avocados, cakes, candies, sodas, ice cream.
2. Drink plenty of water *between* meals to prevent dehydration. Try to limit fluid intake at mealtime to eight ounces to prevent dilution of enzymes and allow for

proper digestion and absorption of the meal. Drink water in moderation throughout the game to help prevent dehydration and muscle fatigue.

What's a Good Snack for Between Games in a Doubleheader?

1. Foods—fresh fruit, fresh vegetables, water- or juice-packed fruit, whole rye crackers, rice cakes, whole wheat pita bread, water-packed tuna fish, hot cereal.
2. Liquids—water, fruit juices without added sugar, vegetable juices.
3. Other—bee pollen mixed in a glass of fruit juice. Pollen is one of nature's richest foods, overflowing with natural vitamins, minerals, and proteins in the proportional amounts so necessary to digestion and assimilation. Local bee pollen is the best—it has long been recommended by doctors as a nutritional supplement for respiratory allergies.

The tough daily schedules of athletes, coaches, and parents make rigid adherence to good nutritional habits difficult. High cost and inconvenience don't help. Be flexible but be smart—considering everything, investing in your body makes good sense; especially when you realize it's the only body you have!

4

Mental Conditioning

Mental conditioning, the least understood of our controllable variables, is a result of combining information and experience with the understanding and controlling emotion to become knowledge. The resulting mental conditioning must take a position on our road to success in a way that best fits the natural ability of each athlete. Personality traits play a big part in successful mental conditioning; it is difficult for an individual to change completely, but there must be enough influence on the mind to allow a young pitcher's physical potential to emerge as consistent performance between the lines.

Coaches and athletes seem to agree that the mental approach of any competitive athlete is the component that contributes the most to career success or failure—assuming that the athlete has the physical talent to perform. As a player, my mental state often influenced my performance, both positively and negatively. I remember two games in particular that can illustrate

my point. Both appearances were similar situations with contending ball clubs: I was a relief pitcher in New York in mid-August, against left-handed hitters of comparable abilities at the top of their game. First let me outline the circumstances that led to my failing performance: It was Red Sox vs. Yankees in Yankee Stadium, a 4–2 lead in the ninth with two out and men on first and second, and Chris Chambliss was the hitter. I came into the game feeling great physically but mentally pressed because the summer hadn't gone well. The Boston fans and media were down on me hard—as only Boston fans and media can be—because I hadn't pitched well all summer. A recent management change hadn't helped, and I was trying to gain Don Zimmer's confidence at the same time I was trying to keep my own. I felt that this game could be a perfect "redeemer" and, coming out of the bullpen, I kept repeating "Just keep him in the yard," meaning don't give up a home run. In our conference on the mound before my warm-up tosses, Zimmer said the same thing: "Anything but a 'dinger' and we win this game. Go after him." My last thought as I began my stretch to deliver the ball was "Don't get this fastball out over the plate or he'll hit a long ball." Well . . . you guessed it. Home run, first pitch.

Now, the successful performance: It was the Braves and the Mets in Shea Stadium, the lead was 3–2 with two men out and the bases loaded in the bottom of the sixth. Rusty Staub was the hitter. I felt a little draggy physically because I had been in three of our last four games, but I felt sharp mentally—aggressive and confident. I could hardly wait to go head on with Staub. This confidence was the result of regular use, solid performance, and an overall belief that I was number one, at least in the Brave bullpen. In our conference on the mound, manager Eddie Mathews said, "Go after him with your curveball. He hasn't got a chance." If you guessed I got him out, you guessed right. I retired Rusty, struck him out, and went on to retire ten men in a row.

In the first example, my physical performance was affected by my strong negative mental image of a home run. My physical performance in the second game was the extension of some strong positive mental imagery. Positive mental conditioning was not the only factor in my successful performance, but at least my mind didn't get in the way of my physical potential. Based on results, there was no external way to see what was right or wrong with my mental state in either situation. A closer internal look showed how my mind contributed to success and failure on the mound.

An athlete's mental state is seldom observable, and uncovering head troubles and dealing with them makes mental conditioning a frustrating variable to work with. The sad thing is, that some kids cannot admit to problems, even to themselves. Others know

that they are having trouble and admit it to themselves, but are embarrassed to admit their problems openly. Still other kids cry wolf all the time and coaches eventually ignore everything that comes out of their mouths. Finally, some kids might have terrible mental problems, but perform better than anyone on the field. This is the "can't miss" prospect who fails on and off the field when he finds competition that challenges his physical ability, when the need for something more than a talented body presents itself. The surprising thing to me is that some athletes perform in major league competition on pure physical ability, with little or no help from mental conditioning! How good could they be if they understood problem tendencies early in their career—not after the fact when forced out of the game or out of the closet and into an alcohol or drug rehabilitation center? My point is, unfortunately, that more fine athletes wash out of baseball because of mental problems than anyone cares to admit. As a coach, it is frustrating to watch.

Everyone admires mental toughness, but few instructors feel qualified to teach it. I believe it can be understood, and it can be taught. The information is available and, short of real psychiatric problems, can be used on the field in a way that helps decrease the failure rate. Athletes and coaches must know that information can be imparted *but* experience *cannot*. Even the brightest young pitcher must match his grasp of information with practical effort between the lines. This is where emotion comes in. As we mentioned in the last chapter, no physical or mental preparation can compensate for uncontrolled emotions. When an adrenaline rush hits with all its accompanying side effects, the world becomes a high-speed video screen, and the athlete who hasn't experienced this often loses contol of his ability to perform. It's different with every pitcher, but usually the kid we call a "gamer" controls it for himself. The kid who can't get it together is usually the one whose emotions control him. His knowledge and physical ability are neutralized when this happens to him.

It doesn't help to treat this syndrome with indifference or embarrassment. It does help to treat the emotional component as you would a muscle. Call it an emotion muscle—it's either strong enough to support the system or it is underdeveloped. It has atrophied and needs work to have enough strength so that it won't detract from the system. The emotion muscle learning/building curve is a personal thing. A coach must recognize problems and discuss them freely and firmly with the athlete. Both coach and athlete must realize that emotional problems have solutions and can be coped with, and that there are tactics to help. For example, automatic responses can take over if a pitcher doesn't have a strong emotional grasp. This boils down to lots of physical repetition from the pitcher and lots of verbal encouragement from the coach. A Pavlovian* response to any game will never take the place of natural athletic reaction, but the two are related and at least it gives a bit of a window to kids whose emotions keep them from effective performance.

For many reasons, the game of baseball does not encourage players to develop emotional strength. Athletes are pampered, admired, and generally allowed to prolong their emotional adolescence. It seems that the stress of being center stage allows players to ignore everyday pressures and duties that build emotional strength.

---

*Ivan P. Pavlov (1849–1936), a Russian physiologist, was the first to describe and study classical conditioning. He used a tuning fork, ringing it every time he fed one of his laboratory dogs. Eventually, he was able to get the dog to salivate at the sound—even when food was nowhere within the animal's sight or smell.

By prolonging adolescence, the maturing process is distorted, creating athletes who must perform tremendous physical feats under intense stress but may lack the mental and emotional makeup to do so. The system does little to counsel and direct players toward emotional maturity. Coaches and athletes are beginning to see that the human mind can be a strong ally or a dreaded enemy—and often both at the same time. Interaction of thought, emotion, and performance under pressure creates an infinite number of variables that can never be completely understood, only observed as trends. Even baseball statistics such as batting averages, ERAs, and fielding percentages just indicate trends by measuring actual performance. Nothing exists to measure potential for performance. For example, there is only one Tom Seaver in baseball. What makes him unique? It's not physical characteristics. Odds are that other people walking the streets may match Seaver's physical body type, strength, and stamina, right down to eye-hand coordination and reaction time. What makes Tom Seaver unique is his mind, the mental and emotional makeup that allows him to be the statistical marvel we have watched for the last 20 years.

Does a star pitcher get scared? Fear success? Fear anything? Just like all of us, the answer is a resounding yes! But how a baseball player handles fear and other problems separates the big winners from the average athletes and from those players who never even become average. The internal and external devices that players use to overcome performance barriers allow their physical potential to emerge as talent on the pitcher's mound. We're going to look at those devices in this chapter.

As you read this part of the book, keep in mind that the high failure rate in baseball has to be caused more by mental problems than by physical shortcomings. There are too many physically superior athletes who don't come close to achieving superior results. Mental problems can be defined as thoughts or emotions that inhibit performance. Realize that performance is relative. Many successful major league pitchers don't reach their best performance because of mental or emotional barriers, but they are still better than their contemporaries. Such misuse of talent means lost opportunity and swaps what "could be" for "what is." Just because a player is good doesn't mean he or his coach should stop trying to improve, trying to reach total potential. Few athletes can afford to stop trying to improve and this chapter is directed toward the athlete that most of us are—one who needs all the mental and emotional toughness he can muster to get by with given physical ability.

Let's get back to the premise that mental and emotional toughness are teachable traits, basically the learning and coordinating of goals, objectives, strategies, and tactics. Learning or knowledge is the product of information coupled with experience; emotion is the "noise" or interruptions of the system. To this, baseball adds exaggerated stress. How would a business executive react to the stresses of his job if his mistakes were all watched by 40,000 people and then printed in the newspaper the next day? I am sure the stress level of his success or failure would jump during his climb up the corporate ladder. Pressure to perform takes on new dimensions when you add an audience. Think about the last speech you gave to a group and about how your mind and body reacted to standing in front of the audience. Fear of failing, letting yourself and your team down, no matter how well they play ups the emotional ante considerably. A pitcher faces this every time he goes to the mound, and we haven't even mentioned personal problems such as family fights, lack of money, illness, flat tires, or any of a million other obstacles we all face every day!

From Little League to major league, every player has had problems with stress, performance, and success. Defining mental conditioning goals and objectives and examining ways to achieve them can help. Understanding, and communicating this understanding becomes our mental conditioning goal. By maximizing our knowledge of who, why, what, and where a pitcher stands intellectually and emotionally, and trying to match this to a physically conditioned and mechanically sound body, we create objectives. Some further definitions, rules of thumb, and miscellaneous information can aid our understanding of a pitcher and his four "W's." Whether they know it or not, most pitchers experience feelings before, during, and after competition. Sometimes their feelings get in the way of performance and if this becomes a habit, there is a problem. The problem is described best as what behavioral science calls dissonance. Dissonance is a vague to profound feeling of mental discomfort about a situation, and three kinds of dissonance can affect a pitcher's athletic life: precompetition, competition, postcompetition.

PRECOMPETITION DISSONANCE

Precompetition dissonance is worrying about something that hasn't happened, and letting that worry affect your performance. It's like stage fright, and I've seen this fear of failure cause pitchers to "freeze up." Negative thoughts about what could happen stops them from achieving maximum performance. It's strange because, when asked up front, few players are afraid to go out and pitch. What they fear is how they will feel after they have gone out to pitch. "What if" becomes a force that impairs "what is."

It seems to help when a pitcher with this problem finds out that everyone has it—it's only a matter of degree. So it helps to get it out in the open and discuss the phenomenon for what it is: a common occurrence among all athletes. Many successful pitchers have precompetition dissonance; but some have learned to cope with the problem. Jim Palmer of the Baltimore Orioles always had pregame complaints about where he hurt—maybe his back or shoulder. Rumor had it that his teammates rated the complaints and found that the worse he felt, the better he pitched. His teammates actually worried when Jim didn't complain! Was this Jim's mind getting him ready for a game? Whatever the reason, there was no doubt about Jim's durability or performance. Focusing thought on something other than fear while preparing for physical performance can lessen apprehension about performance.

COMPETITION DISSONANCE

Competition dissonances are mental blocks that occur because a pitcher's emotion or stress problems won't let him think through a situation and make useful plans. It all boils down to planning your work and working your plan. Have an idea! If you use your knowledge of what can go right and avoid thinking about what can go wrong, you get the most out of physical potential. As we said earlier, knowledge can only be reinforced with experience. A pitcher may have had outstanding coaches, may understand everything, and have total recall of what every situation requires, but until he experiences the process of turning knowledge into physical action, learning isn't complete. Failing to match knowledge with physical action does not make a pitcher a failure. A young pitcher learns from failing and accepting failure is avoided when the athlete and coach find ways to avoid making the same mistake again and again. The key here is information. The more information a pitcher has about the four "W's," the better his chance to overcome mental blocks.

Proven baseball objectives, strategies, and tactics can help a pitcher reach his performance objectives. Remember, it's information, and any information will be interpreted differently by every pitcher. However, the knowledge/experience interaction should result in a better understanding of why something worked or didn't work—the ultimate return coming in improved performance.

A Pitcher's Objectives

- Work purposefully, showing as little emotion as possible. Just appearing to be in control will carry you most of the time.
- Throw what you want to throw—if you can't decide what to throw, step off the mound and start over. The wrong pitch that you believe in is better than the right pitch thrown with less than total commitment.
- Your last thought must be positive—see yourself doing it right, visualize the result you want. Avoid the "I don't want to" syndrome because your last thought is usually the one that affects your physical performance. Not wanting to hang a slider is negative visualization.
- Always believe you are one pitch away from getting out of the worst jam. Pitch to get the hitter. Everything else is secondary.
- Identify your strengths on a given day and do not worry about your "stuff" on the hill. A hitter adjusts to what he sees, not to

how you feel or what you think you are throwing. Changing speeds and location should be adjusted to a particular day. If you can't locate, change speeds, and vice versa. The odds still favor a pitcher who can do either if not both. This is analogous to the pitcher who "coasts" until he gets into a jam, then turns it on.

- Pitch within your abilities. If you demand more of your talent than it can give, you become as inefficient as those pitchers who don't try at all. Work smarter, not harder.

- Your chances of getting a hitter out are much greater when you get ahead of him in the count. To do this, you must throw strikes. Pitch aggressively. You cannot "pick" at the plate and throw strikes consistently. Remember that the guy you are trying to get out is having the same mental battles you are. If you execute your plan, the odds are in your favor—.300 hitters hit .300 on mistakes, not on quality pitches.

STRATEGIES AND TACTICS

- If a hitter stands close to the plate, pitch him away. If a hitter stands off the plate, pitch him in. Batters normally stand in the batter's box to protect their weaknesses. The man who crowds the plate usually is not afraid to be challenged inside or he wouldn't be there. Standing away from the plate suggests that the hitter likes to extend his arms and has no trouble reaching the ball.

- Crouch hitters usually hit the high ball better, stand-up hitters the low ball. They are setting up for a better perspective and tend to exaggerate the set-up to compensate for their weaknesses.

- Pitch a hitter *in* to win. The plate is a

battle zone and if you let a hitter dominate the whole space, he will hurt you eventually. By throwing inside, right under the hands of a hitter when he takes his stance, you can: (1) Stop him from reaching the outside corner without paying the price of intimidation. If he guesses wrong, the ball will go deep into his "kitchen,"* or even hit him. (2) Force him to speed up his bat. This opens the possibility of an off-speed pitch and further increases the difficulty of timing your pitches. The only exception to this strategy is when a hitter can inside out the ball (hit an inside pitch to the opposite field). If you pitch him away and defense him away, half his options are eliminated because most hitters cannot pull an outside pitch effectively—it must be stroked to the opposite field. Not pitching inside restricts the batter's ability to go inside out and both ways with the ball.

- Key your pitch selection and location to bat speed and plate coverage. If a hitter is getting good contact on quality pitch away, then usually he can be pitched hard inside and vice versa. If a hitter is late on anything hard, come right back with another hard pitch placed a little further inside. Conversely, if a batter is "turning" on your best hard stuff, then you must slow his bat down with an off-speed pitch. Remember this—most hitters key on fastball, guess location, and hope they can adjust. You have four choices on every pitch: fast, slow, in, and out. Observe your hitter, look for his tendencies, know what the score and count dictate for your opponent's probable course of action, and work accordingly with pitch selection. No situation exists for a pitcher where some course of action isn't indicated. Exploit it. If a hitter has a known weakness, work it

---

*"Kitchen" is baseball slang for the bat area just below the hands. Pitchers love to get in a hitter's "kitchen," hoping to break the bat.

until he proves he's adjusted. Do not out-think yourself. If a batter cannot hit a breaking ball, don't give him a fastball to hit just because you have thrown five successive sliders. Conversely, if you can overmatch him with a fastball, don't give ⟶⟶⟶ ⟶⟶eed to hit. If you feel ⟶⟶⟶⟶⟶ ifferent pitch, just be ⟶⟶⟶⟶⟶ ate, then come right ⟶⟶ ss.

⟶⟶ e first hitter you face ⟶⟶ y to successful pitch-⟶⟶ ⟶e a favorite mental/⟶⟶ ⟶elp prepare you dur-⟶⟶ ⟶he last of your warm-⟶⟶ t pitch to the lead-off ⟶⟶ ⟶ing a golfer take two ⟶⟶ l, but only counting ⟶⟶ ⟶use the physical and ⟶⟶ ⟶icated so closely, the ⟶⟶ better than the first. ⟶⟶ ⟶tter method, try it. It ⟶⟶ pitcher, and it has ⟶⟶ ⟶g pitchers I have ⟶⟶ of the lead-off hitter

⟶⟶ ⟶jectives, strategies, ⟶⟶ competition disso-⟶⟶ ⟶roach to the game. ⟶⟶ ⟶er comes closer to ⟶⟶ ⟶ental goals and ob-⟶⟶ ⟶rstanding and com-municating who, why, what, and where he is in his intellectual and emotional growth as a pitcher.

POSTCOMPETITION DISSONANCE

Postcompetition dissonance is letting what has already happened adversely affect present mental state. Again, there are no perfect answers to this problem but some thought patterns can direct a pitcher to better ways of tying a ribbon on yesterday's package of perceptions. When something is in the books, dwelling on it is not going to change it. Try to look at what happened as if you were an impartial observer. If you can see it with a realistic attitude, your peaks and valleys won't be as steep. These suggestions might help:

a. If you are still congratulating yourself on yesterday's performance, you haven't tried or done anything today; you haven't prepared yourself for the demands of today's performance.

b. The same is true if you are still punishing yourself mentally or physically because your last effort was poor, or even a failure. A bad experience can also be a learning experience. The key is knowing why you failed. If you don't know why, you probably didn't start with a plan or idea. With no idea, it's impossible to make changes for the next time you experience a similar situation; this increases your chances of committing the same mistake again. You are not growing mentally if you make the same mistake time after time. Plan, react, evaluate, store applicable information, reject superficial information, and get ready for today.

Those are the basic dissonances a pitcher must deal with. Now let me give you an outline to guide your mental conditioning process and help you handle dissonance:

• Set priorities. Know what's important and work toward success with a structured approach.

• Take on your problems. Problems are opportunities in disguise; they are only roadblocks if you allow them to be.

• Set and demand standards of excellence for yourself.

09-16-92
17-15 0037

1   •0•49 I
1   •4•99 I
1   •3•99 I
1   •2•99 I
         •0•50 I   TX
         •12•96 ST
         •20•00 CA   AT
         •7•04 CG

- Work with a sense of urgency. Nothing gets done with procrastination.
- Pay attention to relevant details and ignore everything else.
- Commit yourself and try not to compromise that commitment. Anyone can find an excuse for not following through if they look hard enough.
- Don't waste time worrying about things you cannot control.
- Have the guts to fail. Look at it, examine it, but don't be resigned to failure.
- Be tough with yourself.
- Work with your emotions—try to make them work for you, not against you.
- Have some fun. It's great therapy.

Remember, you don't have to like all the things that help your mental conditioning—you just have to understand them. Be persistent and selfish about using your mind. It must be exercised to grow. Every investment you make in your mind will come in handy in the future. Today's sacrifices provide tomorrow's mental strength. To be a successful pitcher, you need a mind and emotional makeup that won't be shaken by every crisis.

5

The Mechanics of Pitching a Baseball

State-of-the-art information and techniques have made specialized instruction about pitching a baseball possible for the first time in the game's history. Many long-accepted notions on throwing have been changed. It's now known, for instance, that a proper combination of body mechanics and physical conditioning can increase arm speed. Increased arm speed means that the velocity of an athlete's fastball can be improved any time in his career—something once thought impossible. In the past "why" could only be explained by memories of experience. It's still true that nothing replaces experience, but throwing can now be photographed, computerized, even cross-referenced to display a theoretical ideal. Each pitcher is different, but some pitching absolutes hold true for all athletes who throw a baseball and patterning yourself after the ideal can improve your pitching. There is still room for individual interpretation, but understanding the absolutes in-

creases the probability that a pitcher will master the mechanics of his position much earlier in his career.

This chapter is aimed at helping pitchers understand throwing mechanics. We will define concepts and introduce some new vocabulary. Then, actual photographs of pitchers throwing will illustrate clearly what the body does during a delivery.

Throwing is a combination of balance, direction, and weight transfer. Each pitcher should pattern his natural delivery after what is theoretically most efficient and then master the throwing motion through repetition and reinforcement so that muscle memory replaces conscious mental effort. It helps to think of the body as divided exactly in half with the throwing side identified as the "strong" or back side and the glove side as the "directional" or front side. Please read, review, and reread this chapter so that you have a good mental image and can understand the vocabulary and concepts.

STEP-BY-STEP PITCHING

The sequences on the following pages illustrate the step-by-step process of one complete delivery, from starting stance to follow-through.

Don Sutton

Starting stance

Initiating the wind-up

Pivot position

The start forward

Post position

Initiating delivery

Forward stride

Landing of the stride foot

Acceleration of the arm

Forward thrust

Release of the ball

Pronation of the arm

Weight over the leverage leg

Goose Gossage

Starting stance

Initiating the wind-up

Pivot position

The start forward

Post position

Initiating delivery

Forward stride

Landing of the stride foot

Acceleration of the arm

Forward thrust

Release of the ball

Pronation of the arm

Weight over the leverage leg

Dave Dravecky

Starting stance

Initiating the wind-up

Pivot position

The start forward

Post position

Initiating the delivery

Forward stride

Landing of the stride foot

Acceleration of the arm

Forward thrust

Release of the ball

Pronation of the arm

Weight over the leverage leg

THE STARTING STANCE

The starting stance from wind-up position should include the following:

1. Eyes on target.
2. Weight evenly distributed with pivot foot half on, half in front of rubber. (Having total weight on pivot leg makes pitcher susceptible to balks with runner on third. A false break by this runner necessitates a weight shift from pivot foot to back foot to step off the rubber; umpires might see this as the beginning of the wind-up. So keep a balanced stance.)
3. Always hide the ball. Don't find your grip until your hands come together and then keep back of glove up and toward the hitter with ball, fingers, and wrist deep in pocket of glove.
4. Right-handed pitchers (RHP) should work from the right side of the rubber; left-handed pitchers (LHP), from the left side—see diagram on page 71.

Andy Hawkins

Bruce Sutter

Rick Sutcliffe

Do not sacrifice comfort on the rubber, but if you have no foot position preference, try this method because the angle of the pitched ball is more efficient and intimidating to hitters. A fastball gets to the hitter quicker, especially to the low-inside zone because, mathematically, it travels less distance, and a curveball appears to break bigger from the batter's perspective. Put yourself in the batter's shoes in the diagram above for an imaginary look.

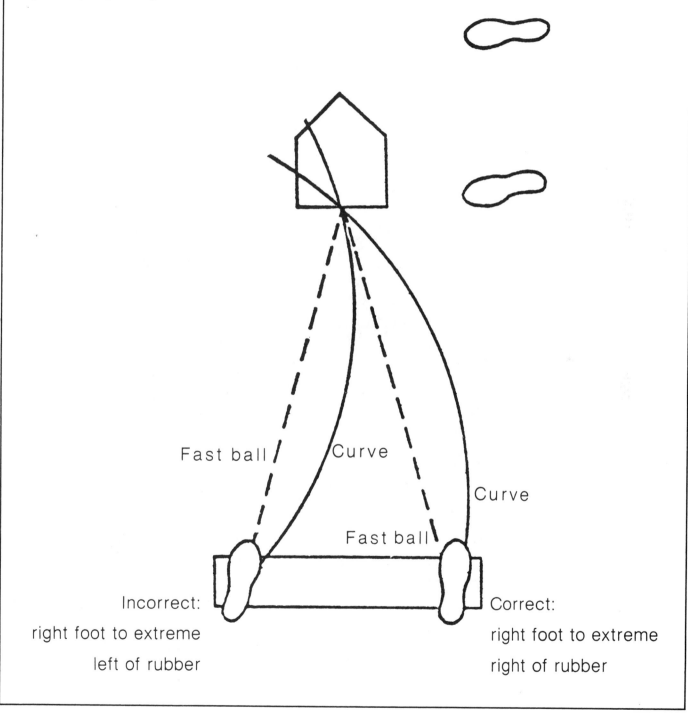

Fast ball

Curve

Curve

Fast ball

Incorrect:

right foot to extreme

left of rubber

Correct:

right foot to extreme

right of rubber

INITIATING THE WIND-UP

Initiating the wind-up properly should include the following:

1. Transfer weight to back foot with a small reverse or side step while comfortably lifting hands as high as pitcher can. Find grip on ball, making sure ball is well hidden in glove.

2. When glove reaches its highest point, place the pivot foot down in front of rubber (*not* on top and *not* half on–half off, but *down in front* to set the beginning for a firm "posting" with pivot leg).
3. Keep head over pivot foot at all times.

Note that the back foot will become part of the pitcher's front or directional side as his delivery continues.

Doyle Alexander

Charlie Hough

Bud Black   Bert Blyleven   Andy Hawkins

THE PIVOT POSITION

The pivot position should go this way:

1. Transfer weight from back foot to posting foot.
2. Back leg begins movement directly to plate, becoming part of directional or front side.

3. Keep head forward of shoulders with chin tucked slightly toward front shoulder on a route directly in line with home plate.
4. Note: throwing from *stretch position* is the same, mechanically, once the pitcher has transferred his weight to the posting foot.

Joe Niekro

Nolan Ryan

Phil Niekro

Bud Black

Doyle Alexander

Bert Blyleven

THE START FORWARD

When starting forward, a pitcher should do the following:

1. Hands and front leg start toward a natural "closing off" or "tuck" position at the *same time*.
2. Shoulders start to line up directly with the home plate.
3. Head stays forward of the shoulders with chin staying close to front shoulder.
4. Start front knee toward the belt buckle by *lifting* with quadriceps. *Do not kick* with this leg at any time—it causes upper body to compensate by leaning back, forcing it off the direct line toward home plate.

Phil Niekro

Rick Sutcliffe

Nolan Ryan

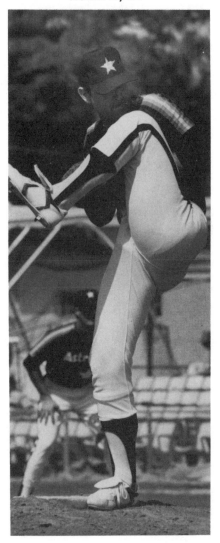

Jeff Reardon

John Tudor

Charlie Hough

THE POST POSITION—ATTAINING BALANCE

The post position is important to good throwing mechanics and should include the following:

1. A solid posting on strong side with the button of pitcher's cap over the ball on his post foot. *Do not* collapse or rock off this post position by bending the post leg excessively. *Do not* lean back from this position with the upper body; keep the shoulders in line with home plate.
2. Close off front or directional side to a "beat" of balance. Let shoulder, hip, and leg close together, like a gate, at an angle that is natural and comfortable—usually to a point right over the rubber.
3. *Do not* start forward with delivery until the front knee reaches its highest point of elevation. Height of knee and length of arm arc are directly related—pitchers with high leg kicks usually take a long arc with throwing arm and vice versa. Adjustments to hold runners close from stretch position can be made after mechanics have been mastered.
4. Try to keep hands together and as close to the chest as possible until the body starts forward. This will prevent the front side from flying open and sets the stage for throwing hand and glove to separate in an action that promotes good direction.

Bud Black

Andy Hawkins

Jeff Reardon

Dave Smith

Bert Blyleven

John Tudor

INITIATING THE DELIVERY

Here's what should happen when delivery begins:

1. After the beat of balance and the closing off of the front or directional side, *begin a controlled fall, not a violent push or drive*, toward home plate.
2. The whole front or directional side takes a firm route toward home plate in a straight line between the pitcher's front shoulder and the catcher's face mask. Keep the head slightly forward of level shoulders and maintain the angle of waist to upper body achieved when direction was begun.
3. Hands break *naturally* with gravity, turning thumbs under to force elbows up.
4. Path of arms is unique to each pitcher within these parameters: With *throwing arm*, wrist stays on top of ball until arm begins forward acceleration. Fingers stay on top throughout delivery on all pitches. Arm swings naturally from shoulder when arm begins its arc on the back side. The angle of front shoulder/back shoulder is also unique to each pitcher because of the way their torsos adjust to lifting their leg. *Front side arm*, extended or bent, must stay directly on line with the throwing arm, until the front foot lands and the throwing arm pushes it out of the way.
5. There is no such thing as a "short armer." The longest any pitcher's arm can be is the distance from shoulder to elbow. No matter what route the throwing arm takes, it stops momentarily just prior to acceleration to home plate—when the arc changes its direction from down and up to forward and through for the throw.

John Tudor

Bert Blyleven

Bud Black

Rick Sutcliffe

Andy Hawkins

Jeff Reardon

THE FORWARD STRIDE

The following things can help you when taking a forward stride:

1. Continue a controlled fall with front foot leading whole directional side toward home plate.
2. The ball swings down, back, and up with the back of wrist to the sky until throwing elbow approaches shoulder height. Concurrently, the front side elbow is approaching shoulder height in *its* route.
3. The whole front side—shoulders, elbow, forearm, hip, leg, and foot—follow a direct route to home plate to prepare for the foot landing and eventual weight transfer.
4. Eyes center on target right over the top of front elbow and glove.

Nolan Ryan

Charlie Hough

Orel Hershiser

Dave Smith

Bud Black

Rick Sutcliffe

LANDING THE STRIDE FOOT

As the stride foot lands:

1. The ball reaches its highest point in arc of arm on pitcher's strong side—*elbow height is even with shoulders.** Front side elbow is *also* shoulder height, setting the stage for an efficient wheeling motion.

_____

*Do not worry about "short armers"—as long as they get the ball to this position efficiently, length of arm arc is incidental.

2. The pivot foot remains in contact with rubber.
3. The stride foot lands in a direct line with target with front knee, hip, shoulder, and elbow following in succession.
4. Shoulders should be as close to level as possible with head slightly forward of body's midpoint and chin buried against front shoulder.
5. Try to keep head as low to ground as possible as stride foot lands.
6. Length of stride should not inhibit weight transfer.

Andy Hawkins

Bud Black

Phil Niekro

Orel Hershiser

John Tudor

Joe Niekro

ARM ACCELERATION

The following points are critical as the arm accelerates to throw the ball:

1. Throwing elbow and frontside elbow stay level with shoulders.*

---
*The same is true for side-armers—they just bend over at the waist to deliver the ball.

2. Pivot foot leaves rubber, and weight is *transferred* to a bending stride leg.
3. Strong side begins replacing directional side en route to home plate.
4. The directional side elbow should remain *at least* as high as the right or strong side elbow and on line directly toward the target until weight transfer occurs and the action/reaction of throwing begins.

Bruce Sutter

Dave Smith

Charlie Hough

John Tudor

Bert Blyleven

Nolan Ryan

THE FORWARD THRUST

With arm thrusting forward correctly to release the ball, the following things occur:

1. Throwing elbow leads throwing arm forward. Throwing is internal rotation of shoulder and elbow.
2. Strong side completely replaces directional side as weight is transferred completely to landing leg. At this point, shoulders pass each other in opposite directions with head becoming an axis for arm's path over a bent (at approximately a 90° angle) knee. This is a point of maximum leverage in the throwing motion.
3. Forearm and wrist of throwing arm are actually parallel to the ground. Glove hand and arm are pulled toward the body *at exactly the same angle* as the throwing arm comes through its arc—sort of a "captain's wheel" action/reaction in a throwing plane that gets maximum arm acceleration with minimal upper body resistance. An axis for this acceleration is created by having the *pitcher's head directly over the maximum leverage position of bend landing leg and knee*—this becomes a critical check point in delivery.
4. Problem areas for this critical check point:
   a. "late" throwing arm due to rushing through balance point, causing front foot to hit prematurely.
   b. "flying open" due to using front side as a power movement.
   c. poor elbow position resulting from improper "posting" over strong back side. (i.e. hands away from body "kicking" the lift leg, etc.).

Andy Hawkins

Orel Hershiser

Doyle Alexander

Joe Niekro

Bud Black

Rick Sutcliffe

RELEASING THE BALL

When the ball is released properly, the following should occur:

1. Head is directly over leverage leg, creating an exit for arms to rotate through in their most efficient angle.
2. Arm snaps to full extension.
3. Wrist is straight and firm behind ball.
4. Fingers are on top of ball—on *all* pitches. Film shows there is only ¾″ difference in finger alignment between a pitcher's biggest breaking curveball and his biggest breaking screwball (theoretically, the two pitches break in opposite directions and are the slowest of pitches in a hurler's repertoire). The grip on ball is important because it affects rotation. Imparting rotation makes ball move. Not everyone can throw the ball hard, but everyone can be taught to make the ball move. See basic grips on following pages.

Bruce Sutter

Rick Sutcliffe

Dave Smith

Orel Hershiser

Charlie Hough

Bud Black

PRONATION OF THE ARM

The following things occur at point of release and right after ball leaves fingertips of throwing arm:

1. Throwing arm snaps straight to full extension at release point.
2. Throwing arm pronates—the palm rotates thumb down and out, away from body—as ball leaves fingertips. This occurs on *all* pitches, breaking balls included (which require supination prior to release point).
3. Weight begins to transfer forward of leverage knee—upper body is actually pulled through by throwing arm. Keep head low to ground.
4. Pivot heel continues to rotate out and up, and foot begins to leave rubber.

Rick Sutcliffe

Charlie Hough

Andy Hawkins

Orel Hershiser

Doyle Alexander

Don Sutton

WEIGHT OVER THE LEVERAGE LEG—WEIGHT TRANSFER

The following actions center the weight of a pitcher's upper body over his leverage leg:

1. Shoulders, arms, and upper body extend and pivot around the axis created by pitcher's head over his leverage leg.

2. Back leg comes off the rubber to counterbalance the upper body extension toward home plate.

3. The more extension a pitcher gets after releasing the ball, the better his upper body absorbs and dissipates the shock of throwing.

4. Balance over landing leg is only important until the arm has decelerated.

Orel Hershiser

Rick Sutcliffe

94

Bert Blyleven

Dave Smith

John Tudor

Joe Niekro

THE FOLLOW-THROUGH

The following things occur in a pitcher's follow-through (Remember, there is no follow-through if weight transfer doesn't clear in front of leverage leg after ball is thrown. Watch for a recoiling action—if this occurs, the pitcher's stride is too long.):

1. Throwing shoulder has driven toward target, completing replacement of directional side with strong back side.
2. Arm pronates and begins deceleration.
3. Upper torso extends to absorb shock of slowing arm down.
4. Back side leg lifts off rubber to balance the process.
   a. Most sore or hurt shoulders occur during deceleration of arm. Mechanically, three muscle groups are involved in acceleration but only one muscle group in deceleration—reinforcement is needed for building strength and flexibility.
   b. The better the balance from back side leg, the more extension is achieved and the better the upper body can absorb and distribute the shock of the throwing arm slowing down.
5. Get the whole body under control and become an infielder with defensive responsibilities.

Andy Hawkins

Bruce Sutter

Jeff Reardon

Nolan Ryan

Joe Niekro

John Tudor

PITCH GRIP BIOMECHANICS

Your grip on a baseball is the final factor in your implementation of a quality pitch. Being efficient, effective, and putting rotation on the ball at the release point requires an overall command of body mechanics: good balance, proper direction, and adequate weight transfer. It specifically requires that the front (or directional) elbow and the throwing elbow be on line with the target, and at least shoulder height as the front foot hits and the throwing arm accelerates to deliver the ball. Assuming that these basics are in place, there are some other absolutes which affect grip and rotation on the ball:

1. The throwing arm rotates internally as it accelerates, it snaps perfectly straight at the release point, and pronates in deceleration on *all* pitches.

2. Arm position from elbow to shoulder is the same on every pitch, no matter what the pitch is. It is the arm position from elbow to finger tips which accounts for the spin on the ball. Therefore, the spin that makes the ball move is a function of forearm/wrist position and proper finger placement over the top of the ball at the release point.

3. The grip from which all pitches key is a cross seam fastball grip. This is a maximum velocity, maximum force pitch requiring that the total body stay behind the ball with forearm, wrist, and finger tips (especially the middle finger) imparting rotation directly through the middle of the ball. The palm of the hand is facing directly at the target at the release point. The ball, using the face of a clock for reference, would have a reverse "12 to 6" spin.

4. To make the ball cut, slide, or curve requires increasing degrees of supination by forearm and wrist (supination means accelerating the forearm and wrist in a "karate chop"-like action with the palm facing inward, toward the body). At the release point, the finger tips of your index and especially the middle finger are to the left* of the center of the ball. The more supination, the further from center the middle finger is, and the more spin is generated over the upper left part of the ball as it is released. Ideally, arm speed is the same as with a fastball—the force of the finger tips on the ball is directed off of center, or over, instead of through the ball. The seams should have a forward "11 to 5" spin.

5. To make the ball run, sink, or screw requires increasing degrees of pronation by forearm and wrist. (Pronation means accelerating the wrist and forearm with the palm facing out, away from the body, leading with the thumb side of the hand). At the release point, the finger tips of the index and especially the middle finger are on top of, but to the right of center of the ball. The more pronation, the further from center the middle finger gets and the more spin is generated over the upper right region of the ball as it is released. Ideally, arm speed is the same as with a fastball—the force of the finger tips on the ball is directed off of center, or over, instead of through the ball. The seams should have a forward, "1 to 7" spin.

6. A change-up is a pitch that is gripped to minimize the force exerted by the finger tips on the ball at the release point, while still maintaining arm speed. There are numerous grips—from splitting the fingers to "choking" the ball back in the hand. Final choice for a change grip is a function of comfort, feel, and command. *Any* grip that maintains arm speed and minimizes the force (therefore the veloc-

---

*If you are right-handed, reverse this.

98

ity) imparted to the ball at the release point, will work.

Finally it is worth repeating that there is only ¾" difference in finger placement over the top of the ball between the biggest curve ball and the biggest screwball, theoretically the two extremes of a pitcher's movement/action repetoire. Velocity always decreases as the middle finger is moved away from the center of the ball and there is no *true* grip for any pitch—it is a function of hand size and comfort. The grips shown here are only starting points. These are traditional finger placements on seams to show you the basics so that you can determine what works best for you.

THE BASIC GRIPS

Fastball

Fingertips on a seam, thumb underneath on a seam, grip firmly with fingers but have a loose wrist. Ball should "rip" out of fingers to get maximum rotation. We all can't throw hard, but everyone is capable of making the ball move.

Fastball, across four seams

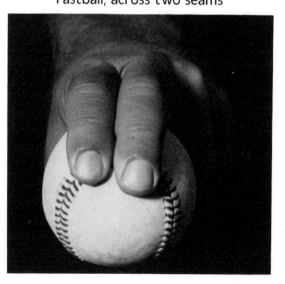
Fastball, across two seams

Fastball, with seams

Curveball

Middle finger next to seam. Index finger supports. Thumb underneath to get the most rotation at release point. (Same as snapping fingers except ball is between thumb and fingertips.) Curve is an off-speed pitch—it will not break properly if thrown too hard. Impart rotation while thinking, "How easily can I throw this curve and still get it to home plate." Arm position same as fastball with wrist and forearm supinating to allow fingertips to snap over the top of the ball.

Curveball

Slider/Cut Fastball

Tip of middle finger should be on a seam, thumb underneath. Slider is a power pitch—the only difference between it and a fastball is that middle finger "cuts" through the ball at release point, wrist is slightly off center.

Slider, off two seams

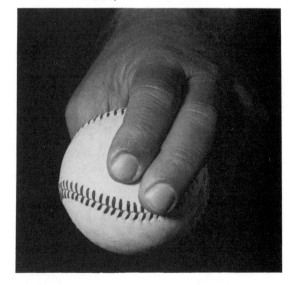

Slider, off four seams

Change-up

Fingertips *off* the seam, ball arranged to come out of hands as *inefficiently* as possible with same arm speed as fastball. Look for less velocity first, movement second. Usually splitting fingers or "burying" ball deeper in hand will accomplish a lesser velocity goal.

One more thing: pitching is a "ballet" of balance, direction, and weight transfer. A solid delivery requires rote skill, that is, muscle memory that will carry on despite the unpredictable physical and emotional swings caused by variable game conditions. Your performance potential cannot be turned into physical performance if your skill is marginal.

Split finger

Palmed changeup

"OK" changeup

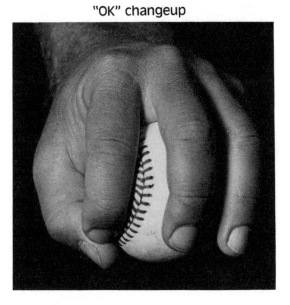

Little League changeup

The beginning of the breaking ball. This gives youngsters a second pitch that will not hurt their arms. Using this grip, throw the ball as if it were a football spiraling at release point.

FIELDING MECHANICS

A pitcher is a defensive player before and after throwing the ball to home plate, so the mechanics of fielding the position are important. A good fielding pitcher can significantly increase his chances of winning. Good defense is just applying basic rules, techniques, and physical positioning during a game. It doesn't require superior athletic ability, only understanding the "why"—then working pitchers fielding practice (PFP) until you can react without having to think out an action as it happens during a game. Requirements are very traditional, and except for minor rule changes and individual interpretations, they have been the same for decades. In the following situations, we will discuss the basics of PFP. Fine-tuning them will be left to the athlete and coach in their workout sessions.

Comebackers to the Mound—No One on Base

1. Catch the ball.
2. Follow your glove toward first base to get proper direction.
3. Crow hop/step to initiate momentum.
4. Throw the ball.

Covering First Base—Ground Ball to First Baseman

1. Get body under control after follow-through.
2. Teach yourself to break toward first on *every* ball hit to the right side of the diamond, whether it's a ground ball, fly ball, line drive, whatever. . . .
3. Take a direct line from that point to the cut of the grass or approximately 10′ to the home plate side of the bag; go as hard as you can to that zone.
4. Get your body under control with short,

choppy steps and ask for the ball early; it's difficult to catch and toss and touch the bag simultaneously.
5. Touch the inside $\frac{1}{3}$ of the bag with the right foot.
6. Clear the base and pivot, following your glove toward the infield in anticipation of another play, even with no one on base. Make it a habit, and you won't forget when there *is* a runner already on base.

Double Plays

1. Know who is covering before you even step on rubber.
2. Hold runner close. A pick-off move is really a "hold close" move.
3. Catch the ball hit back at you.
4. Follow your glove toward second for direction. Pick up covering infielder in your line of vision.
5. Crow hop/step to initiate movement, especially if you are going back "up" the mound.
6. Throw the ball quickly. Lead the infielder if he is late getting there (like a receiver in football). The quicker you unload the ball, the better your chances of turning two.

Pick-Off Move

1. RHP must clear feet with throw to first. Throw should be quick rather than hard—keeping elbow close to hip will help this.
2. RHP should *lift* the leg directly to where the front side closes off to balance. Lifting and rotating takes too long to unload and kicking the leg forces upper body to come off balance point. A RHP should try to get the ball delivered to home plate in 1 to 1.2 seconds—but don't sacrifice good stuff for a quick release. The hitter is the primary concern.
3. A LHP has an advantage because he faces the runner. If he just closes off his front side properly, it will freeze most

runners. Good base runners go on first movement with LHP anyway, so it's becoming more of a guessing game. Beyond that, the following rules apply:

- The pitcher's front foot cannot break the plane of the rubber. If it does, pitcher must go to home plate with the ball.
- If the pitcher comes to first, he must step toward the bag at an angle of 45 degrees or less.

4. LHP should throw over a lot and never give a bad move to set up a good one. The runner may be lazy, especially if he has no intention of going. Throwing over often diminishes the chance of guessing right on a steal. It helps take away the opposing team's running game.

5. A LHP should lock head and look at a zone between home and first. This eliminates the problem of looking home and throwing to first or looking to first and throwing home (which enables the runner to predict and guess correctly when to steal). Peripheral vision tracks both the target and the runner.

6. Both RHP and LHP should vary the timing of their delivery and always make the runner stop before throwing home.

Bunting

There are numerous plays and defensive alignments for all bunting situations—individual managers and coaches will use their favorites. In all cases, however, the following techniques apply.

1. Charge the ball with rear end as low to the ground as possible.
2. Arrange feet before reaching the ball.
3. Field ball out in front of body, not between legs—two hands if the ball is moving, bare-handed if the ball is stopped.
4. Follow your glove toward the direction you are throwing.
5. Crow hop/step and throw.

Backing Up Bases

This is not difficult, and can eliminate giving up extra bases or free runs if done consistently during a season.

1. Back up one base ahead of where you think the runner could end up. So for a sure double, back up third and for a sure triple, back up home. If the ball is in a gap with runners on base, drift in the area between third and home until the play develops and make your decision accordingly.
2. Back up behind the bag as deeply as possible in a direct line with the incoming throw to aid the angle of pursuit if the ball gets by the infielder at the bag.

PRACTICING THE MECHANICS

Pitching mechanics, both throwing and fielding, are probably the most easily mastered of our three controllable variables. When explained and understood, they are rudimentary. Feedback is instantaneous, and mastery requires only enough physical repetition to match the skill to an athlete's ability. It goes almost without saying that the better conditioned a pitcher is mentally and physically, the more effectively he will apply skill to the mechanics of pitching in games.

We have now discussed the three controllable variables I think are most important to a pitcher's career. It would be wonderful to say that these things alone can make you succeed. Unfortunately, there are no guarantees and you can only increase your *chances* of succeeding. For the committed athlete who wants success badly enough, that's plenty. You should keep in mind that uncontrollable variables can skew the direction of any career. We'll discuss some of them briefly in the next chapter.

6

Vision Dynamics—the Concept of Centering

For this chapter, I have asked Dr. Bill Harrison—a friend and experienced sports theorist—to share his views. He has some unique insights to help you round out your understanding of "self" and the game we call baseball.

It was a warm and not too hazy October afternoon in California, a great day for a picnic or a ball game. In Dodger Stadium, 56,242 shirt-sleeved people were gathered in the sun—not for a picnic, but for the fourth game of the 1981 World Series, Yankees versus Dodgers. It was big-time baseball, draped in red, white, and Howard Cosell.

Things looked bad for the Dodgers. Trailing in the series two games to one, they were also behind 6–3 in the bottom of the sixth in this game. In 56 games during the regular season in which the Yankees were leading going into the last three innings, they had lost only *once*. It was bleak for the Dodgers.

On the mound for the Yankees was reliever Ron Davis, definitely no slouch out of the bullpen. He'd come in to pitch in the bottom of the fifth, ending a Dodger rally by striking out Dusty Baker and Rick Monday as if they had lead in their bats. During the season, Davis had tied a major league record by striking out eight consecutive hitters. In postseason playoffs, he'd simply been overpowering.

After retiring the first hitter in the bottom of the sixth on a feeble grounder, Davis had a temporary lapse, walking the next batter, Mike Scioscia. That brought up pinch hitter Jay Johnstone. Davis straddled the rubber, peering in to get his sign from catcher Rick Cerone. They both knew the book on Johnstone; he'd been their teammate two years before. A free swinger, he was up there looking for a fastball about belt high, something he could jack out of the park and get the Dodgers back in the game. Ron knew the way to pitch him—hard stuff either away, or up and in, or with sliders on his fists. Davis wasn't about to try to get cute. A power pitcher, he would challenge Johnstone with smoke. Cosell called it a 94-mph fastball; hitters refer to it as "cheese." In other words, Johnstone couldn't go up there swinging a slow bat or it would be three quick ones.

Checking the runner on first, Davis let fire with his first pitch. The ball sizzled into Cerone's mitt, a perfectly called strike, low and away. Johnstone's bat never moved. Wasting little time, Davis toed the rubber again, then cranked another express toward the plate. Johnstone uncoiled with a hefty cut, but he was overmatched. His swing was about a foot late. In the one-to-one battle between pitcher and batter, there is nothing as ego-building for the pitcher than to blow the ball right past the hitter.

After wasting a pitch outside, Davis stepped back off the mound and turned his back to the plate. He took off his cap to wipe his forehead and adjust his glasses. He thought about the pitch he wanted to make. He wanted a strikeout, or better yet, a ground-ball double play.

Stepping back onto the mound, he checked his sign from Cerone again, then came set. It was to be a fastball, down and away. But this time, instead of popping into Cerone's mitt for strike three, the ball sailed right down the middle of the plate. Johnstone's eyes lit up like a kid in a toy store. His bat exploded off his shoulder, and the ball rocketed into the right field bleachers faster than you can spell c-o-n-c-e-n-t-r-a-t-i-o-n. The Dodgers were back in the game. The next hitter, Davey Lopes, lofted a high fly to right field. Yankee outfielder Reggie Jackson, looking up into the bright sky, staggered, and the ball bounded off his chest for a double. Unnerved, Davis fell apart on the mound, letting Lopes steal third without so much as a nod. One pitch later, a single brought him home with the tying run. That was all she wrote for Davis, and as it turned out, it was also the end of the Yankees in the 1981 World Series. Davis finished up the series with a disastrous 23.140 ERA. Several months later, he was to lose his salary arbitration hearing for $600,000, forced to settle for significantly less.

So what happened? Why did Davis's first two pitches to Johnstone zing right into the catcher's mitt—just like they were supposed to—but just sixty seconds later why did he serve up a cream puff right into Johnstone's wheelhouse? After the game, as he slumped on the stool in front of his locker, surrounded by dozens of sportswriters, Davis tried to explain. "I just made a bad pitch," he said, shrugging his shoulders. But why? He could study films of the pitch until Babe Ruth came back to life, looking for a mechanical flaw in his delivery. He might even find what he was looking for, a release point $\frac{7}{12}$th of an inch higher than it should have been. But so what? Every big league pitcher worth his agent knows the mechanics it takes to make the right pitches. So do the hitters. It's the execution of those pitches that counts when the chips are on the arbitration table. Fernando Valenzuela can roll his eyes to the skies when he's in his wind-up, defying every bit of instructional advice since Abner Doubleday, but somehow he pulls it off. The key is *concentration*. Pitching is perhaps the most challenging position in baseball. Not only must fundamentals and techniques be proper and effective, but the mental aspect of pitching is perhaps more demanding than in any other sport.

As a pitcher, you face a new challenge on every hitter and almost every pitch. The time delay between pitches and hitters makes it very difficult to maintain the same mental level throughout every pitch, inning, and game in the season. All kinds of personalities are successful at pitching—solid citizens, competitive and aggressive individuals, coaches' dreams, and a wide variety of oddballs, screwballs, and goofballs. Even for pitchers with the best physical ability, it takes time, practice, coaching, and experience to master the fundamentals of pitching, then learn to execute these skills under the pressure of competition. But where do fundamentals really begin? Do they begin when the pitcher puts his toe on the rubber? Or are there fundamentals that come before that? I think there are several basic areas that deserve attention, basic mental fundamentals that can be improved regardless of your stage of development.

CONSISTENCY IS THE KEY

The areas that we want to focus on are designed for one purpose: to improve your ability to *consistently* perform successfully under pressure. To be a pitcher, you undoubtedly have a lot of physical skill, and as long as you pitch, you will be working on refinement of the proper fundamentals of pitching. But your overall success is going to be determined by the consistency with which you pitch under pressure. That consistency, in my opinion, is a byproduct of the proper mental approach that works for you. If you have had any success in pitching, or perhaps in any other sports, the answers for your success lie within. Keep in mind that what works for you may not be the same as what works for the next guy. Certainly you have to be willing to experiment with other approaches, particularly if you know an approach that has been successful for someone else. But in the final analysis, your mental approach to pitching must be based on an approach you've had success with.

ANALYZING YOUR SUCCESS

One of the best ways to gain insight into how you have performed in the past is to recreate in your mind a series of past successes. I want you to compare your successes with your failures, and let's determine just what goes into a consistently good performance for you.

Close your eyes and imagine a day when you pitched exceptionally well. Think of specific games or perhaps certain innings or hitters you pitched to effectively. Think of the times you had good control, command of your pitches, and felt as though you had mastery of the game. As you are thinking, visualize the game as vividly as possible. See your opponents, the weather, the crowd, the color of the opponents' uniforms, how your body felt, and the emotions. Before going further in this chapter, turn the book over and take some time to think about your pitching successes. If you haven't had much success in game situations, think about instances in the bullpen when you had command of your pitches. Even if you have to think back a few years to a lower level of ball, think about the times that you were truly king of the mound.

Now that you have reflected on your best performances, answer true or false to the following statements:

- You had a clear visual picture of exactly how you were going to throw each pitch.
- Your concentration was on the task at hand—throwing the ball to the target.
- You weren't thinking about making your body, or a part of it, go through the pitching motion. You just did it.
- You were highly aware of seeing your target, but the hitters and everything else were just a faint blur.
- Your mind was out of your body as if it

were following the ball into the target.
- There were no distractions.
- Time slowed down so that you had plenty of time to think and/or do what you wanted.

Now that you have thought vividly of your successes and responded "true" or "false" to the above statements, how do you feel mentally and physically? Where would your confidence be if you had the chance to go out and pitch right now? I expect you have that good feeling, that high level of confidence. The emotions, the feelings that you have now are a result of using your mind effectively to visualize your successes. As mentioned earlier, many answers to your successes lie within you, within your mind, but you must use your mind properly to find the answers.

Although I believe in a positive approach to pitching and that we can learn from our successes, it is also helpful to analyze our failures. Most pitchers and coaches spend an incredible amount of time and energy searching for the "whys" of poor performance, but I question that approach. Good, accurate feedback is necessary to improve or learn any sport. If feedback is not accurate, it can lead you down a path to nowhere.

Let's consider the simple game of darts. How would you perform at darts if you were blindfolded? You could execute good mechanics and fundamentals and fire the dart toward a target, but if you don't get any feedback on how close you were to the target or by how much you missed it, how could you plan your next toss? Think about it. Do you think you would become more accurate at tossing the dart even if you had 100 tosses? Sure, you might get lucky and get close to the center of the target now and again, but would you bet money that you could throw a strike? And without doubt, during the 100 or so tosses, you would

demonstrate a variety of faulty mechanics. You would rarely take the same physical approach and your mechanics would look poor. And your body certainly would play back some poor feeling—tightness, awareness of body parts, poor rhythm and timing. No matter how much you practiced mechanics and fundamentals, probably you would improve only a small amount, because no mental game plan and no target exists. As a point of clarification, the drilling mechanics and fundamentals would be handy later when you develop the proper mental game plan, but without a game plan, your performance would be inconsistent. Getting feedback from poor performance is not simply analyzing your mechanics and the inner feelings of your body but accurately analyzing your mental approach.

ANALYZING YOUR PITCHING PROBLEMS

Let's look at some of your poorer pitching performances. Again, visualize game situations vividly—the teams, the weather conditions, the crowd, your emotions, how your body felt. Think about different hitters, situations, and specific innings. Again, turn the book over and recreate your poorer performances in your mind. Now answer true or false to the following statements:

- You did not have a clear visual picture of exactly what you wanted to do with each pitch and how you wanted to throw it.
- You thought about what you didn't want to do—like not walking a guy, not hanging a curveball, not wasting a pitch too far outside.
- You were highly aware of some part of your body as if you were steering that part of the body through the motion.
- Your concentration was on previous

pitches or situations, on future pitches or situations, or on things totally unrelated to the game.

● You cannot recall seeing your target when you were into your motion or throwing the pitch.

If you answered true to most of these statements about when you were pitching successfully and when you were pitching poorly, you are like most athletes. I've worked with top performers in baseball, football, golf, skiing, tennis, and hockey, and they answer the above statements almost always the same. To be consistently successful you need to control concentration, control and use visualization, have a heightened awareness of what your eyes are seeing, and control the energy system so that the body reacts with good rhythm and timing.

CONCENTRATION

Visual-mental skills can be learned just as easily as physical skills—reading, writing, or throwing various pitches. But like reading, writing, and throwing a certain pitch, these skills require practice and training. The more you put into it, the more you get out of it; but by putting anything into it, however small, it will teach you something. Proper grip, arm action, and body mechanics are extremely important and must be worked on and refined constantly. But so must the fundamentals of concentration, visualization, and proper use of the eyes. It may seem like a lot, but no one said this game would be easy. It takes a lot of work, but the work pays off in big dividends. There have been many talented pitchers with strong arms who never made it to the point of consistently good performance. In the 1960s Larry Colton was the hottest pitching prospect the Philadelphia Phillies

had, a certified "can't miss" player. He had a bazooka for an arm, a bright head on his shoulders, and big bucks in his future. But Larry never made it. As he explained:

"I used to sit in the dugout and watch other pitchers go out to the mound with half the stuff I had and win consistently. I'd shake my head and wonder why they could do it and I couldn't. It had to be concentration. These guys blocked out everything else in their lives but the catcher's target. An A-bomb could have gone off in center field and they wouldn't have known. Not me, my mind was all over the place. I'd stand on the mound thinking about the price of eggs or what some jerk behind third base was yelling out. I remember one night in San Diego in July of 1968. It was late in the game, and I was trying to protect a one-run lead. There was a runner on second. As I stood on the mound getting the sign, the crowd started to cheer. I couldn't figure out what it was all about. I stepped off the rubber, thinking my pants had split open or the runner had collapsed, or something. But it wasn't any of those things. Nope, the fans were cheering the message on the big board above the right field seats. In huge neon lights, the message read, 'Hubert Humphrey wins Democratic nomination.' I stood there shaking my head, mad as could be. I wanted McCarthy, even going so far as to put a peace emblem on the rear window of my car, which in baseball circles in those days was the same as being a commie or pinko. The louder the cheering got, the madder I became. When I finally climbed back on the mound, the batter drilled my first pitch halfway to Tijuana, and I lost the game. That sort of thing happened to me all the time. I'd lose my concentration, thinking about anything but the task at hand. Once, after an argument with my wife, I pitched the whole first inning in a semi-rage, thinking about all the things I wished I'd said to her. I kept looking up into the stands where she was sitting. In the second inning, I didn't have to worry about it. I didn't last that long . . . I was knocked out of the box."

I'm sure every pitcher can think of similar situations. Lack of concentration can make a potential top performer into a mediocre player. Concentration can also make a pitcher with marginal physical ability perform better than athletes with superior physical skills. But concentration is the elusive butterfly of all sports. When you have it, everything seems easy; when you don't, no amount of effort seems to bring it back.

What is concentration? If you were my coach and told me to concentrate, what would you say if I asked what you meant? And if I asked you to teach me how to concentrate; how would you go about it? Isn't it interesting that we generally think about the word "concentration" only when we don't have it? Most attempts to master concentration involve trying to block things out, trying harder, gritting our teeth, or bearing down. Taken literally, these approaches translate into increased energy output that alters your rhythm, timing, fine muscle control, balance. Paradoxically, concentration is best when you are not trying to concentrate: when you are concentrating properly, you are usually unaware of it. Good concentration rarely results in *trying* to concentrate.

Concentration is a description of the end result of doing something rather than a description of *how* to do it. Nevertheless, concentration can be learned, and it can improve your performance greatly. Many pitchers have had great success learning to control concentration with a physical process we call "centering." Centering is what concentration is all about.

CENTERING

To understand how centering works, tune into the background noises around you. Perhaps you can hear someone talking, a baby crying, a bird chirping, street noises in the distance, the hum of an air conditioner. Now shift your attention to your clothing. Can you feel your collar, your shoes, your sleeves? Take your time. As you shift to your clothing, what happens to the background sounds? Do they fade for an instant? Notice that as you center in on one system, the other fades into the background. This process of selective attention is centering. Do you ever drive down the highway and suddenly realize that you missed your turnoff miles back? Do you ever read a page and nothing registers? Think of the games when you were getting ready to pitch, looking at the catcher, but your mind was on something off the baseball field. You were still centering, but not on pitching, and that resulted in poor concentration. The point is that you are always centering. You can center on a thought, something you see, hear, touch, feel, taste, or smell—but you can only center on one thing at a time. Of course, you can shift so quickly from one thing to another that it seems as though you are centered on more than one thing at a time. That's similar to watching television for an hour but changing channels every five seconds. At the end of the hour you could say that you burned a lot of energy watching television—you tried hard, bore down, but nothing registered.

Centering has nothing to do with trying hard. It is simply an active process of attending to information through one of your senses or through a thought. When you pitched at your peak, it was probably as if your mind were in the present. That is, you only centered on what was happening at the time. You did not think about earlier plays or future concerns at the time you were in action. Between hitters, when the action stopped, you may have shifted your attention to something relaxing—the clouds overhead, a tree in the distance, and, yes, the pretty girls in the stands. But when the hitter was in the box, your attention was totally on getting your job done. That is a sort of centering, and learning to control that skill can help you focus your concentration on the present, no matter what the conditions of the game are.

Not only must you center on the proper system, you must center to the proper degree. You can center broadly, taking in as much information as possible, or you can "fine center," where you channel your attention toward a very small area. Directing your centering toward the webbing on the catcher's glove, a scratch on his knee guard, or the stitching or insignia on his sleeve is fine centering. When you fine center a target with your eyes, everything else blurs and fades away. The opposite of fine centering, "space centering," focuses more broadly. You literally space out. Your mind drifts and rarely stays on one thing for any length of time. Think about when you throw the ball most accurately—do you space center or fine center? Even when you think about other sports, you're likely to find that you've been most accurate in your kicking, throwing, hitting, or touching when you have been fine centered on a target. There is no right way to do it, the best way for you to center lies within you.

What degree of centering has been most consistently successful in the past? What was your target? To reach the concentration that makes you a consistent top performer you must learn how to stay centered on your target, and you must also determine accurately what that target is.

TARGET SELECTION

Target selection is simple if you ask yourself what your job is as a pitcher. Most pitchers answer that their job is winning, striking out the hitter, or not giving up any runs. But those are really goals, desirable but not the target for our centering. No matter what circumstances exist, the pitcher's job is always the same. Whether it's Little League tryouts or the seventh game in the World Series, you must throw the ball to a target. That target may be the catcher's glove, mask, knee guard, or it may be a visual zone over home plate. In the bullpen warming up or in workouts between games or spring training, it's a totally different situation. If you or your coach determine that you need to work on a position, for example, then you had better be centered exclusively on the body awareness system. And your criterion of success should be whether you executed the shoulder turn properly—not whether you threw the ball to the target. I find that when most pitchers say they are working on mechanics, they think about the mechanics they are going to focus on, but when they go into the motion and release the ball, they are not centering on the specific fundamental, but are just space centering generally on what they feel and the target they see. And the result is the "grooving" of poor mechanics. It is important that you work on mechanics and fundamentals, so when you do . . . do it. Isolate a specific fundamental and center on it. Do not be concerned with the accuracy or quality of your pitch. Even if you throw the ball over the backstop, a properly executed fundamental will ultimately help your effectiveness. The task at hand? To center on the fundamental and develop it so that it becomes a proper and natural reaction.

When you center on one part of your

body, the rest of the body will not flow with proper rhythm and timing. But you improve that particular fundamental movement. The results of your efforts are not judged by your ability to throw quality pitches to a target when you are on the mound, in a game, and allowing your body just to react. If your body doesn't react with good mechanics, you must return to the bullpen for more attention to fundamentals. And, while you must specifically center on them, your practice session in the bullpen must include specific attention to the mental game plan you will use in the same situation the next time out.

In the bullpen, you should practice centering on different targets. Determine if you get better results by looking at the target from the beginning to the end of your delivery or by spot centering on the target— looking away during part of your motion, then looking back at the target just before delivery. Perhaps what works best at one time may change as your experience and concentration skills increase. Develop a game plan. Although the score and the situation varies, you need a game plan to stay tuned in to each shot. After all, in game conditions your job is always the same: throw the ball to a target. That task never varies despite the score or playing conditions so you need a plan to follow, one that is workable whether you feel strong or weak, up or down, and whether you're winning or losing.

A STEP-BY-STEP APPROACH

Here is a plan that can help you develop a consistent approach to the game, help you get more out of your workouts, and learn more from your game experiences. Like any physical performance, practice is necessary to tap the potential resources of the approach. When developed properly through practice, the approach becomes a natural reflex and you will automatically use it to approach the game. Before each pitch, go through these steps:

- *Analyze the situation.* This step is straightforward, but if you don't incorporate it into your game plan, you're doomed for inconsistency. Survey the game situation, the score, the count, the outs, the base runners, and analyze the hitter. Determine the best pitch to make, but also think about what the batter is likely to be looking for before making your final pitch selection. Also, think about fielding situations that you may have to react to. Part of this step takes place before the catcher gives the sign and part of it after you agree to a certain pitch.

- *Visualize and energize the pitch you are going to make.* You must experiment in the bullpen and learn from game situations how to do this most effectively. The minimum would be to visualize the last 15 to 20 feet of the pitch you expect to throw, seeing its final trajectory. The quality of your visualization will have a direct impact on the value of this step, so attempt to visualize clearly, including the spin of the particular pitch. With experience you will be able to visualize the complete pitching motion, with proper mechanics and the great feeling of a flow of energy through your body. The visualization of the pitching motion will then flow into the trajectory of the pitch going all the way to the target.

- *Fine center on the target.* Pinpoint your centering on the smallest target that works for you. Fine centering does not mean tightening or aiming the ball; although you are fine centering with your mind, just let your body flow to the target.

It should seem as though you are connected to your target by an invisible funnel and, as the pitch is released, you should be so centered that you follow the ball right into the target. It's as if your centering directs and controls your energies.

- *Execute.* Proper execution comes from having the basic skills, understanding fundamentals and techniques, visualizing the correct performance, and centering on the target.

- *Playback.* This is the most important step to master if you want to be a consistent top performer: after each pitch, decide whether you analyzed, visualized, and centered properly. It takes more than good intentions; you have to do it. Make it a habit, particularly in the bullpen, to visualize the previous pitch from start to finish. Play back exactly what you centered on to examine the quality and accuracy of your prepitch visualization, and you will play back where your centering was during the pitch. This will show you what centering gets the best results and, if

there was a breakdown in your centering control, what led to the physical or fundamental mistake. Often the reason your performance broke down was improper centering. By adjusting your centering, you get back to the execution of proper fundamentals with the next pitch.

Now you have a basic game plan that you can tailor to your needs. You will probably adjust it as you get future pitching experience, but you should use a game plan for every pitch if you want to be consistently successful and able to perform under pressure. *Winning is important. But you can't control who wins; you can only control yourself and make certain that you give it the best you have.* Win as often as possible. The best you have will probably lead to winning, at least as often as is possible for you. It will keep you in the game and give you the chance to win. It will give the feeling you did your best. Skill is not an accident of birth. It can be developed through training. This approach promises no miracles but it can help you reach the peak of your individual performance.

Acknowledgments

Special thanks to all the pitchers who agreed to be featured in this book. They're all different in their methods, but they all agree on one thing: you need more than a strong arm. It takes plenty of hard work, patience, and determination to be a pitcher.

So the next time you see one of these men pitch, or you happen to pass their plaque in the Hall of Fame, just remember this: it doesn't happen overnight. I just hope this book will help it to happen faster.

—Tom House

Rick Sutcliffe: Power and deception.

Nolan Ryan: Perhaps the hardest thrower ever.

Andy Hawkins: Don't be fooled by the "nice guy" image; he'll blow you out of the box.

John Tudor: Gets batters to hit grounders on the turf.

Bert Blyleven: The best curveballer around.

Orel Hershiser: Nice guys *don't* finish last.

Don Sutton: The Trickster—created variations on everything.

Goose Gossage: The Intimidator.

Dave Dravecky: Best cut fastball in the league; sheer determination.

Bruce Sutter: His split-fingered fastball revolutionized the game.

Doyle Alexander: The Deceiver.

Charlie Hough: One of the few remaining knuckleballers.

Bud Black: The curveball specialist.

Phil Niekro: The infamous knuckleballer.

Joe Niekro: Followed his big brother's footsteps.

Jeff Reardon: The Terminator.

Dave Smith: Split-fingered fire out of the bullpen.

INDEX